ECONOCRACY:
Paradigm for Africa's Development

*Scribble*City
PUBLICATIONS

DEDICATION

To the evergreen memory of PHILOMINA, my mother whose (immense) love for me and loss at a tender age defined and continues to define the trajectory of my life.

ACKNOWLEDGMENTS

I owe my inspiration first to God Almighty as always, then to the pioneer political philosophers whose thoughts on the sociology of politics set me thinking from my days as an undergraduate. Such great thinkers as Plato, Aristotle and other ones that came after them, will always remain my point of inspiration for thought-provoking political formulations like the one on Econocracy and in my first two books: *Reinventing Nigeria: The Plebiscitarian Option* and *Election Finance and Corruption in Nigeria: The Investment Theory Approach*.

Yet, I must confess that great African thinkers such as Frantz Fanon, Chinweizu, W. E. B Bois and Kwame Nkrumah, also set me thinking. Their thought-provoking discourses made me envision that with well thought out political formulations, the seemingly intractable political challenges that have continued to weigh down and draw back African nations since decolonisation, may afterall be surmountable.

I doff my hat for all these great thinkers whose brilliant treatise on political systems helped to build my confidence to think of a possible novel political system for an endangered African continent.

I acknowledge in a special way my long-standing professional colleague and friend, Ifeanyi Iwuofor, who goes by the pen name Pita Okute, for helping me to sharpen the conceptual frameworks of this book. I recall the fateful day I sat with him at a garden in Abuja three years ago and asked him directly what he thought of a novel on political ideology that centres on economic rights, as against liberal rights, as the centroid of African democracy. We discussed at length and that discussion set the template for further thoughts on Econocracy as the paradigm for Africa's development. Ifeanyi was also ready when I called on him to proofread this book. I cannot thank him enough.

I also will not forget to acknowledge Chinwe Ononuju, who helped in many other invaluable ways to facilitate the publishing of the book. I say thank you.

My deep gratitude also goes to my good friend, Daniel Okechukwu, who does not begrudge me for making him my unofficial private secretary. He has always translated my difficult long hand into neatly typed manuscripts, for all my three books. I cannot truly place value on his contributions to the success of my books.

To my wife, Adaobi Maryclaret, I thank her immensely for her encouragements, particularly for providing a peaceful domestic environment that waters my flow of thought.

To Christopher Ebubechukwu Emelumba, my Son, I say a big thank you for having the courage to critique your father's thoughts. Your observations were very helpful.

FOREWORD

Like many other potential readers of this book, the concept of "Econocracy" is novel to me. In truth, I only became acquainted with the concept of Econocracy after the author approached me to write the foreword to this book, "*Econocracy: Paradigm for Africa's Development*". As I read the manuscript and familiarised myself with the term, its origins and the author's rather unique and original thoughts on the subject, I became increasingly convinced that I was perusing a document of genuine political and economic significance to the issue of development in Africa.

This book does not only present a unique African perspective on Econocracy, but also offers a radical re-definition and understanding of the concept as found in the 1975 book, *Econocrats and the Policy Process: Politics and Philosophy of Cost-benefit Analysis* by Peter Self, and popularised by Joe Earle, Cahal Moran and Zach Ward-Perkins in their book, *The Econocracy: The Perils of Leaving Economics to the Experts*. The conceptualization of Econocracy in the aforementioned books is rooted in doubtful concerns over the expertise of professional economics and its ubiquitous presence and influence on public life. Thus, Econocracy is defined as 'a society in which political goals are defined in terms of their effect on the economy which is believed to be a distinct system with its own logic that requires experts to manage it'. This book however, presents Econocracy as a system of economic determination of political objectives, whereby the economic needs and aspirations of the people, as determined by them, not politicians, should form the basis of policy-making. Thus, grassroots economic needs should inform and determine the outputs of the political superstructure.

While this perspective and approach to understanding Econocracy may be both novel and idealistic, it nevertheless provides a comprehensive set of distinctive customized prescriptions covering issues of economic rights and political tenures as a workable pathway to the reinvigoration of African economies which have been seriously stagnated by colonial economic and political models. An extensive review of classical and contemporary political philosophies, establishes the authors idea of Econocracy as a superior recommendation particularly suited to the realities and dynamics of African economies and political systems.

The book further offers an audacious, but compelling justification for the repudiation of Western style liberal democracy, as a desirable political goal in Africa at this point in the continent's quest for meaningful development, prioritizing instead the pursuit of economic rights guaranteed by law as the fundamental objective of government. According to the author, liberal democracy is a luxury Africa cannot afford now, given the prevailing reality of its current socio-economic exigencies.

In this book, the author has raised many questions, and offered answers that grant a deeply insightful appreciation of key issues. The book, "*Econocracy: Paradigm for Africa's Development*" merits a place amongst the different intellectual works put forward recently by scholars and thinkers as a way out of the economic woes that currently limit the development of the African continent. This book will certainly become a handy companion for students, researchers, policy makers and 'the people' seeking sustainable solutions to the challenges of Africa's development.

Professor Bennett C. Nwanguma
University of Nigeria, Nsukka

TABLE OF CONTENTS

ECONOCRACY: ECONOMIC DEMOCRACY

On a trip to a conference in one of the West African countries, while waiting to board a flight, some people started discussing the effects of today's politics; how the politics of today has not helped the economic growth of many countries in Africa. Coincidentally, on my trip back, I sat with a political science research student who sought my opinion on the economic policymaking of a country becoming a technocratic process. As I pondered this in my mind, I knew this would be achievable in a nation where the main purpose of its politics is to improve the economy of the nation, i.e. prioritizing the management of the economy which will also require experts handling major affairs.

I had the privilege of being part of a discussant in a Forum that debated the extent technocracy has gone in the current democratic dispensation in Africa. In this debate, the word Econocracy was used very often as they discussed the current perils of the lack of proficient governance in most of these countries. One of the teams, comparing developed, developing and underdeveloped nations, demonstrated how deficiency of intellectual heterogeneity can be detrimental to the democracy and economy of a country. The other team argued that Econocracy should only be possible and best where citizens possess necessary and prerequisite level of economic knowledge, that will enable them to make knowledgeable decisions about persons best to represent their political and economic interests. Since most African countries are still classified as underdeveloped and developing nations, they argued that people will be exploited in an econocratic system. Their argument stems from the belief that in Econocracy, the masses are not fully involved since policymaking and governance are left to experts thereby depriving the masses from participating and deliberating in their democratic system.

People's viewpoints about this matter intrigued me greatly. All these experiences and more contributed to my conviction to write this book.

Chapter 1

DEVELOPMENT: SCOPE & ESSENCE

The place to begin is to first understand what development really means. Thereafter we can determine to what extent development has taken or is taking place in Africa, and if Econocracy is the pathway to development in Africa or not.

We are first going to examine, then contrast some developed nations with the African nations. The differences discovered from the study will further underscore the underdevelopment status of African countries. In addressing the question of development in Africa, nations are used as units of analysis, although the title of this book may create the impression that Africa is lumped together as one unit. The assumption that informs the reference to the African continent as one unit, is based on their common colonial history and similar underdevelopment challenges. This clarification is necessary because in defining development, I shall be doing so in the context of nations.

National development can be measured in terms of the ability of any given nation to improve on the living standards of her citizens within a given time. For instance, a ten-year period. Thus we can measure the national development of country A or B by improvements in the quality of life of citizens within that period. Areas of improvement on the people's lives that can reflect national development will include provision of social amenities, healthcare, affordable housing, access to technology and poverty reduction. When the lives of the citizens improve significantly in these areas, then development can be said to have taken place nationally. Likewise, when the citizens' wellbeing regularly reflects sustainable improvement in these areas, then the nation is said to be developed. A nation whose citizens enjoy good education, good infrastructural facilities, good healthcare, prosperity, good and affordable housing, as well as advanced technology, is said to be developed.

The degree to which these amenities are available, differ from nation to nation, depending on their productive capacity. Nations with automated and high productive capacity are usually classified as industrialized and developed while the ones with low productivity are classified as underdeveloped or developing. National productive capacity is calculated as a measure of the aggregated value-added output of the economy, which economists refer to as the Gross Domestic Product (GDP) of a country.

Table 1: *IMF World Economic Outlook*

World GDP Ranking [1/3]
GDP in current prices (billions of US dollars) during 2019

#	Country	GDP	#	Country	GDP
1	United States	21,439	23	Thailand	529
2	China	14,140	24	Sweden	529
3	Japan	5,154	25	Belgium	518
4	Germany	3,863	26	Iran	459
5	India	2,936	27	Austria	448
6	United Kingdom	2,744	28	Nigeria	447
7	France	2,707	29	Argentina	445
8	Italy	1,989	30	Norway	418
9	Brazil	1,847	31	United Arab Emirates	406
10	Canada	1,731	32	Israel	388
11	Russia	1,638	33	Ireland	385
12	South Korea	1,630	34	Hong Kong SAR China	373
13	Spain	1,398	35	Malaysia	365
14	Australia	1,376	36	Singapore	363
15	Mexico	1,274	37	South Africa	359
16	Indonesia	1,112	38	Philippines	357
17	Netherlands	902	39	Denmark	347
18	Saudi Arabia	779	40	Colombia	328
19	Turkey	744	41	Bangladesh	317
20	Switzerland	715	42	Egypt	302
21	Taiwan	586	43	Chile	294
22	Poland	566	44	Pakistan	284

Data Source: IMF World Economic Outlook, October 2019

Note: Country name color code:: Advanced economies: Blue, Developing economies: Blac

45	Finland		270
46	Vietnam		262
47	Czech Republic		247
48	Romania		244
49	Portugal		236
50	Peru		229
51	Iraq		224
52	Greece		214
53	New Zealand		205
54	Qatar		192
55	Algeria		173
56	Hungary		170
57	Kazakhstan		170
58	Ukraine		150
59	Kuwait		138
60	Morocco		119
61	Ecuador		108
62	Slovak Republic		107
63	Puerto Rico		100
64	Kenya		99
65	Angola		92
66	Ethiopia		91

For developed nations, they need to sustain annual GDP growth at a certain percentage to avoid decline in productivity. Developing countries must also sustain an annual GDP growth to a certain percentage, to be seen to be truly developing. Development can also be looked at from the perspective of per capita income in a country. The per capita income also gives an insight into the level of development or underdevelopment of a country.

Since national development is all about improving the quality of lives of citizens with respect to the provision of the amenities we have outlined earlier, we shall look more closely at them for a deeper appreciation of their role in national development.

Without proper education, the citizenry will be unable to acquire necessary tools for productive employment. The more educated citizens are, the more skilled workforce there will be in the labour market. Most technological inventions are products of education and research. Only through education can nations make breakthroughs in technological inventions, which in turn drive industrial capacity and expansion. It is indisputable that mass access to education is a facilitator of national development. Education avails the citizens the opportunity for increased skills, creativity and self-discipline. All these attributes contribute to national productivity.

In his book, (Rodney, 1972) looks at national development from the perspective of improving individual skills. He argues that the achievement of any personal development is very much tied in with the society as a whole. According to him, "Freedom, responsibility, skill, etc., have real meaning only in terms of the relations of men in society." The point is that a nation should help, through its programmes and policies, to encourage massive development of skills and creative capacity of individuals. When this is done, the country then becomes more productive in all spheres of life, which translates practically to development.

National development is an economic issue. It is about production and wealth creation. All the indicators we listed earlier help to grow GDP or per capita income. The lesson here is that economic needs ought to occupy the prime place in a nation's development efforts. The whole essence of development is to improve the wellbeing of the people. Put differently, the welfare of the people is at the centre of every development dream. Any national development effort that does not make the wellbeing of the citizens a priority, will be an aberration. Increased productivity measured through GDP or per capita income is seen from an economic telescope, because it is the aggregate of the productive capacity of a nation that determines better housing, better healthcare, better telecommunications, etc. All these are expected to improve the living conditions of the people, which is the factor that determines whether or not a nation is developed.

What appears indisputable is that economic needs should define political objectives. Since nations are considered successful (developed) or unsuccessful (underdeveloped) by the standard of living or quality of life of the people, which is primarily an economic issue, the economic needs of the people should consequently determine what the political objectives of a nation should be. This is more so for underdeveloped nations, such as African countries.

The current practice wherein politics determines economic objectives in African nations is tantamount to building a house by first mounting the roof after which the blocks are fixed from the roof to foundation. This flawed approach is the bane of African development efforts. African nations use politics to define their economic objectives and it has not worked.

Politics here is the process of electing those who govern the nations in a democratic tradition, which involves free, fair, and credible elections. The assumption is that through this process, the people will freely elect credible leaders, who are their true representatives, and who are consequently in a good stead to feel their pulse and determine their economic needs. In Western countries, with high literacy levels bound together by a common language or culture, and appreciable political awareness, such may be accomplished. Indeed, more often than not, elected governments of these countries reasonably reflect the wishes and aspirations of the people. To an appreciable extent, their leaders can be said to be true representatives of their people.

In addition, in most Western nations, the economic needs of the people have been fought for and enforced over time by the people themselves, through numerous revolutionary battles. Those demands can be summarized as free enterprise, dignity of labour, and decent livelihood. The governments of these nations determine the economic needs of the people, within the broad perspective of these three areas, which have long been settled over time. In this case, politics can drive economic needs.

However, the African scenario is completely different. The credibility of the electoral process has remained elusive. Mass illiteracy remains an issue. In addition, diversity of language and culture breeds mutual suspicion. Worst of all, real participation in the electoral process is low. What follows is that those elected into government cannot, in the strict sense of it, be said to be reasonably representing the wishes and aspirations of the people. In such a situation, using politics to define and drive economic empowerment of the people, will be akin to the case of building a house from the roof top. What will follow will be more of a gamble or guess work, that will never succeed in completing the building from the roof to the foundation.

Nigeria's experience with the many failed development plans, support my position on this issue. Two years after independence in 1960, Nigeria rolled out an ambitious development plan that she hoped would see to the rapid development of the country. Among other objectives of the plan for growth was to create ample opportunities in the health sector, improve conducive environment for mass education and expand employment opportunities. The plan failed. There was no evidence, four years after, in 1966, when the military took over government, that progress was made in executing any of the objectives. Paucity of funds was cited as part of the reason for the failure.

(Ogwumike, 1995) is of the view that the plan failed because only fourteen percent of the funds needed from external sources for the execution of the plan was realized.

Not daunted by the failure of the first plan, Nigeria's leaders rolled out yet another ambitious development plan immediately after the civil war in 1970. This was a four-year development plan to last from 1970 to 1974. The objectives were to boost agriculture, facilitate industrial growth, improve manpower capacity, transportation, enhance defence potentials, provide electricity, communication, and water supply. This was a far more ambitious plan than the 1962 plan.

The new plan was silent on the objectives of the 1962 plan in such areas as health, education and employment opportunities. This would suggest that their 1962 objective had already been achieved, which was far from correct. What the silence actually reflected, in my view, was a clear disconnect between past and present development planning strategies. It was a manifest evidence of the absence of continuity in the planning process. The second plan did not succeed either. By the end of 1974, there was nothing to suggest that any of the objectives were met. It appeared that what mattered to Nigeria was the rolling out of development plans with no connectivity in between them or evidence of success. (Ogwumike, 1995) reveals further that a third plan was launched in 1975, covering another five-year period of 1975 – 1980. The priorities of the plan were to encourage rural development and boost agricultural production. The next plan came in 1981 and covered the period 1981 – 1985. This plan again brought the issue of healthcare to the front burner. The plan specifically targeted improving the living conditions of Nigerians by increasing the real income of citizens, ensuring an even distribution of income within individuals and groups, as well as creating employment opportunities (similar objectives to the 1962 plan).

The question here should not be whether these development plans succeeded, but rather why they failed.

The fact that the plans lacked cohesive connectivity, leaves the impression that they were more of a gamble or guess work. Each administration that came, simply rolled out its own vision of development, without as much as looking back to see what happened in the past. The plans were also not based on the knowledge of what the people needed, but on the assumption of what they needed – a classic case of using politics to determine the economic needs of the people.

(Mimiko, 2017) captured this position vividly in noting that the development plans failed *"because there was little or no consultation of the general public. Planning is supposed to involve even peasants in the villages. Even the local government officials, who were closer to the people, were not consulted. Planning is not an edifice where technocrats alone operate."* This is the crux of the issue as well as the soul of my Econocracy model. The lynchpin of Econocracy is about the inevitability of allowing the people, including the peasants, to determine their economic needs for the political class to implement. Details on this shall be provided in subsequent chapters of this book.

Perhaps, even a more pertinent revelation from the failure of these development plans is the non-representativeness of the political leaders who rolled them out. There were leaders who emerged through an imposed colonial political culture, the culture of liberal democracy, which effectively alienates them from the people. As I will explain in the course of this book, liberal democracy is more concerned with the protection of political, civil and social freedom, such as freedom of speech, association etc., because it is a product of the culture of a people who have already secured their economic rights through many revolutions, both bloody and peaceful. The colonial masters simply bequeathed liberalism to African leaders without the technology for its manufacture and the leaders accepted same without questioning. This ensured that from the onset, that there was a disconnect between the political leadership and the people. The political leaders were simply the black variants of the colonial masters. The leaders inherited and sustained a neo-colonial economy that was only too glad to continue to feed their capitalist outposts in the home economies of their former colonial empires, with raw materials from Africa, while eagerly awaiting the finished products, to quench their appetite for foreign goods.

From the point of view of both economics and politics, post-colonial African leadership can best be described as willing apologists of a neo-colonial political and economic superstructure. In the words of (Mimiko, 2017), *"These leaders, on assumption of power, quickly turned up the repressive machinery of the colonial state rather than dismantling it. Significantly, they had no vision of development to accompany the efficient instrument of repression they inherited. All they were interested in was access to power and privileges and not development."* This is the bottom-line. It is not peculiar to Nigeria. It is applicable to virtually all African nations.

What (Mimiko, 2017) words echo is the tragedy of the failure of post-colonial African political leaders who found it inexcusably convenient to forget that Africa had her own history of productive progression. Every society progressed from one productive stage of life to the other and Africa was no exception. The basic challenge of mankind, at the primitive stage of life, was to master his environment and device ways and means of self-preservation, by finding food to quench his hunger, shielding himself from the harsh effects of the weather through shelter, and remaining healthy by warding off diseases through medication. These challenges were the same in every society and man's response saw his pace through the broad progressive stages of primitive agrarian and industrial ages. Africa, even if she moved at a different pace or speed, would have come to the same end, which is industrialization.

Colonialism thwarted and deconstructed Africa's progression. At the point of the advent of the colonialists, Europe had an edge in the progression line because the continent was already a fledging capitalist zone while

Africa was still at the communal stage of development.

Rodney (36) underscores this point vividly by noting that Africa's underdevelopment in relation to the West and a few other parts of the world was arrived at not *"by separate evolution of Africa on the one hand and Europe on the other but by exploitation."* He believes that contact between different societies changes their respective rates of development. It is evident that this was the case with Africa. There is evidence that African societies were progressing, even if slowly, from primitive to the industrial age before colonialism disrupted it. As Rodney (382) recalls, in the area of fine arts, African achievements, of the pre-European period, stands as contributions to man's heritage of beautiful creations. He cited the Egyptian, the Sudanese and Ethiopian arts, which were well known to the world at an early date, as evidence.

One distinctive feature of African societies before the coming of Europeans was that they co-existed based on communalism, that is a pattern of social relationships based on family and kinship, associated with communalism. Every member of an African society had his relationship defined through the extended family arrangement both on his father's and mother's sides.

Rodney (41) further notes that, *"similar social institutions were to be found among the Gauls of the 11th century*

France, among the Viets of Indo-China at the same date, and virtually everywhere else in the world at one time or another because communalism is one phase through which all human society passed." If all human society passed through communalism, which was dominated by subsistence agrarian economy and Western countries later progressed from that age to the industrial age, it makes sense to argue that African societies, without interruption, would have still moved from that age, even if belatedly, to the industrial age. The history of mankind is a record of man's transition from one stage to another. Europe moved from communalism to feudalism and then to capitalism. Each stage threw up fresh challenges for man, and his struggle to overcome them led to the next stage. Africa may not have exactly transited from communalism to feudalism and capitalism, but they would have transited, nonetheless, from communalism to another stage. It was the interruption of colonialism that halted this natural transition process.

At this point, there is a need to refresh our minds that colonialism was a European onslaught on Africa, motivated only by selfish desires. Europeans had a trading relationship with Africa for over 400 years, until the middle of the 19th century, when they decided to take over African societies by force, through the Berlin Conference of 1884. That decision was fired by their desperate desires to support the industrial revolution in Europe with unhindered flow of raw materials from Africa, extracted on their terms and at very cheap rates. There was also the desire to secure safe market for the export of their finished products. Based on these desires, agriculture was encouraged in Africa to produce raw materials for onward export to Europe to feed their industries. (Kato, 1975) observed that in colonial Africa, *"there were huge agricultural plantations with a single production, they were either owned by the colonial government or absent capitalists in Europe, who sent representatives to take over the plantations."*

The more pertinent point to note, however, is that colonialism wilfully set out to dismantle African economic development. Among the ways they accomplished this was by forcefully replacing African traders, with trading companies they established, to handle export/import trade with Europe. African traders were equally prohibited from engaging in various trading activities along the coast of Tanganyika and West Africa, according to (Kamili, 2011).

Perhaps the most divesting drawback effect of European colonialism on African productive energy, was the flooding of African market with European goods, which were better packaged and more attractive.

Consequently, Africans began to see their own goods as inferior and subsequently abandoned them for European goods. It can be canvassed, going by all these, that holistic effect of colonialism on Africa was the imposition of European stage of development on her people. That means that the colonialist imposed their stage on the transition line on Africa, thereby disrupting and deconstructing her natural transition process. Unfortunately, post-colonial African leaders accepted this deconstruction without much ado. The tragic consequence is that they keep trying to develop African countries from the rooftop, where the European colonialist had made them believe they had reached. The result is the disjointed and disconnected development plans they keep rolling out, which keep collapsing like packs of cards. The problem with this scenario is that the real people are alienated in the process. When you talk about employment for instance, it does not take into cognizance the real employment needs of the rural African, whose employment expectations might just be an opportunity to farm, improve on his native textile making or even blacksmithing craft, etc. If they are recognized and encouraged, they could aggregate to a cluster that can ignite technological breakthroughs in the future.

These boils down to the fact that allowing politics to define or determine the economic needs of the people will only lead to the kind of merry-go-round situation we have seen in Nigeria, where development plans were rolled out for mere political glamour, with neither the capacity for its implementation nor the intent to push it through.

Worst of all, such an arrangement ends up proposing plans that are in total disconnect with the economic needs of the people. This explains why African nations have remained largely underdeveloped.

The point to emphasize is the fact that the African situation demands a different approach to development which must be people-oriented. The people should be allowed to identify their economic needs and the political class made to implement them. A necessary component in this respect is mass education. Education is both the foundation and key to the development strides of East Asian countries, namely Singapore, Hong Kong, Japan, Taiwan. These countries owe their development to mass education policies.

It is not a surprise that developing countries, some of which were also ravaged by the exploitative fangs of colonialism, have been able to maintain strong and consistent development growth spanning over five decades.

This brings us back to the meaning and scope of development. From all facts adduced while trying to understand or define development, a few salient points need reiterating. Foremost is that development is about the people, about development of the people to make their lives better and more productive. It is about better living conditions for the people within the context of a nation. This can be extended further to imply that since it is all about people, and in the case of the African people, whose interests are not reasonably reflected in the political class, the people should define their economic needs which should form the substantial part of the political agenda of their nation. This, no doubt, will rekindle the African communal spirit, which was stifled by a rude colonial intervention. It will equally help in bringing back the people as relevant stakeholders in national development. The present disposition of the average African poor is to see themselves as having no stake in governance, and the alarming spate of corruption among the leaders is not helping their waning confidence in government institutions. Liberal democracy, which African nations appear to have become stuck with, is essentially, an imperialist instrument for protecting the capitalist interest in post-colonial African nations.

The next chapter will throw more light on this. Econocracy proposes a more direct involvement of the people in the development efforts of African nations as a means of purging the toxic effect of unbridled liberalism on the democratic institutions of African nations.

Chapter 2

WHAT IS ECONOCRACY?

The concept of Econocracy is not a particularly popular one. Actually, I had not run into the word in any literature before conceptualizing it. For quite some time, over a year or so, I had tinkered with the idea of fashioning out the best pathway for African development until the idea of Econocracy hit me. I had to search for any available literature to see if what I was conceptualizing had any foundation. I found little, except for what I saw in the book by Joe Earle, Cahal Moran and Zach Ward-Perkins, which used the same expression – Econocracy, but offered the opposite interpretation of my concept (Joe Earle, 2016).

In the book, "The Econocracy: The Perils of leaving Economics to the Experts," the authors were only concerned that society was imperilled because we are living in an econocracy. By this, they meant that political goals were expressed in terms of their effect on the economy because economic policy-making is viewed as a technical, not a political activity. For the authors, the main worry appears to be that "areas of political life are increasingly delegated to experts, whether at the Bank of England, the government's behavioural insight team, the competition or the treasury."

There is, however, a meeting point between the Econocracy concept of the authors and mine. The common denominator here is that both concepts, and others I shall refer to later, agree that it means economic democracy; its focus is not on re-politicizing economic system but a people-driven socio-economic system that sets economic agenda for the State to implement.

I define Econocracy to mean economic determination of political objectives. In other words, the economic needs of the people determine politics, not politics determining the economic needs of the people. This will imply that in a given political set up, the people should first identify their economic needs, which should in turn drive the political superstructure.

Let me expatiate on this. Let us take a given society or nation as a country – YZ, with a population of 50 million people. Of course, this population is made up of different segments of people living in different locations with peculiar environmental, geographical and social variables. These variables determine their economic needs.

By econocratic order, each group shall be allowed to identify and articulate their economic needs. The aggregate of these needs from the different groups, will form the national economic agenda. The political structure will consequently be employed to actualize the economic agenda of the different groups. This means that it is not politics that will determine the economic needs of the people but the people themselves. Once this is achieved, politics is compelled, by law, to implement the expressed economic agenda of the people.

Coming back to our country, YZ, let us assume that the different groups in the country identify and articulate their economic needs as food, shelter, employment, good health and good roads. The next stage will be for the political system to be compelled, by law, to implement these needs as the business of government. This we can represent graphically in diagram 1.

Diagram 1: *Political Structure and Economic Needs*

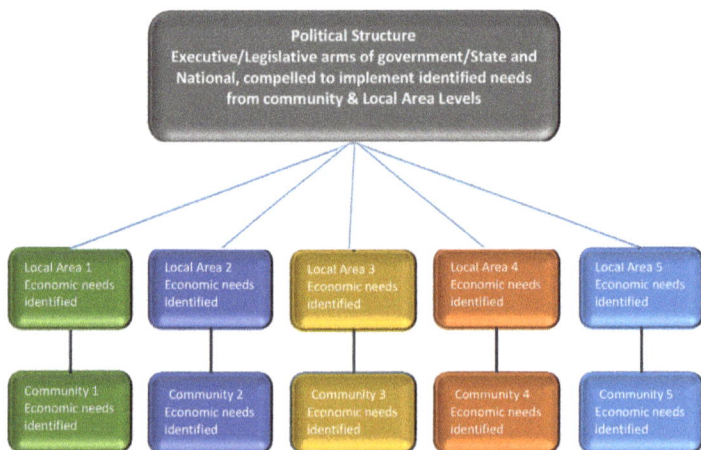

The question may be asked why an elected government should be under force of law to implement the economic agenda drawn up by the people as its policy. This could imply that the government would only be a rubber stamp, without the initiative of its own. My response is that in more advanced climes, where most of the basic needs of man – food, shelter, employment, and good health – have been substantially addressed, Econocracy may not find a recommendation. In such countries, especially countries in the industrialized Western hemisphere, because these basic needs have been substantially provided, emphasis is more on social and liberal rights, such as freedom of speech and assembly/association, gender equality, the rule of law, etc. In Africa and other developing nations, the glaring reality of the excruciating poverty of the people demand that the economic needs of the people should determine the focus of politics.

Liberal democracy, a subject I shall dwell extensively on in the next chapter, is a luxury that poverty-stricken African nations can ill-afford. As a representative government elected by voters, its major defect is that in most cases, those who vote to choose the government are less than 50% of the population. Eligible voters are usually chosen from those of adult age. By this alone, a substantial segment of the population is disenfranchised by law. In addition, not all citizens within adult suffrage register to vote and not all who register to vote actually do so. The practical consequence is that more often than not, less than 30% of the total population, that is, actual voters drawn from the list of registered voters determine who governs the country. This can readily pass as modified aristocracy, christened democracy. The situation is worse in African countries where widespread illiteracy and political docility further shrink the percentage of those who determine those who govern. It is important to emphasize the point at this stage, that liberal democracy wittingly or unwittingly promotes the imposition of the will of the minority on the majority.

This may not be an issue in industrialized countries because basic human needs are already provided for the people. For African countries, where these needs are still begging for attention, it is both an issue and a distraction. I shall get back to this subject in later chapters. For now, let us return to the attempt at outlining the meaning and essence of Econocracy.

Let me put the issue by way of a question: what are the novelties of Econocracy that recommend it to the African situation? The concept suits the African situation because its emphasis is on the economic rights of the individual rather than on civil rights, civil liberties, and political freedom. It promotes an economic superstructure that should drive the political structure. Emphasis is placed on the fundamental economic rights of the citizen which should be guaranteed in the statues as inalienable and non-negotiable. Given the excruciating poverty that has continued to ravage Africa from colonial to post-colonial years, nothing should be spared, in putting in place, an arrangement that facilitates economic growth and development. Econocracy holds a strong promise in this direction.

These rights shall be expressly stated to include rights to shelter, rights to education, rights to skill acquisition and employment, rights to good health and rights to infrastructure. Let me examine each in some detail, so we can fully appreciate what Econocracy stands for.

Right to Shelter

Each citizen shall be entitled to the right to a place of abode, a roof over his or her head. This is not to suggest in any way that the government should provide free homes for every citizen. The provision makes it mandatory for the government to provide both the enabling environment for each citizen to own a home and access to mortgage facilities. Enabling environment will require that the government should make it mandatory for employers of labour to provide a mortgage plan that can afford a home for their workers. Efforts should also be made to ensure that as many self-employed people as possible are captured under a government-backed mortgage for home ownership. No one should be under any illusion that it shall be possible, at any given point, for every citizen to own a home. However, the least that the enactment of this right into law can achieve, is to make both citizens and government conscious of the fact that everyone, as of rights, deserves a home. No doubt, this will make it possible for more citizens to afford homes and enforce their rights to home ownership. In the present situation, where such rights are neither emphasized nor guaranteed by law, the people are forced to live on the streets and under bridges without empathy from the government. In the industrialized Western liberal democracies, revolutions and social pressure across history have seen to it that facilities for home ownership are accessible to and affordable by many. Cautionary measures, by capitalist-driven economies of the West, to avert further pressure on their investment equally helps in providing homes for the people.

Right to Skill Education

What is the worth of an individual that has no value to contribute to his society? Nothing, of course. However, more often than not, the individual is not to blame for his or her worthlessness. Every person has inherent aptitude for one skill or another which, if not developed, can remain latent till death. A lot of difference is made in the life of a person depending on where he or she was born. A child born in Brass village in Bayelsa State of Nigeria, by Mr. and Mrs. B, and grows up in Nigeria, will be remarkably different from the one born and raised in Maryland, in the United States, by Mr. and Mrs. C. Even if Mr. C is of the same biological parentage with Mr. B. The one born and nurtured in the United States is more likely to grow up with more skills than the one born and raised in Nigeria.

Many factors account for this. Nigeria and United States offer different socialization prospects. While the US environment has many outlets for self-actualization, such as facilities for functional education, self-motivation, and skill acquisition, the Nigerian environment does not offer the same. Public education and instructional facilities in Nigeria are in deplorable conditions and it is not likely that an average child can have the full benefits of education through the process. The story is the same in most African countries. So, while the Western countries can afford to take the citizens right to education for granted, African countries cannot and should not.

Why is education and/or skill acquisition an economic right? Without any skill, a citizen will lack self-confidence and esteem, knowing that he has practically nothing to contribute to society. Such a citizen is, in real terms, unemployable. At best, he or she may find employment, if any, only for menial, non-skilled jobs, such as a gateman, a cleaner, etc. Purposeful education can impart meaningful skills in the citizenry for productive enterprise. In the circumstance, functional education that should produce graduates with competitive skills become a fundamental right of the citizen. African nations should promote education as compulsory and free at all levels, terminating with a degree or certificate and a skill to show for it. This will imply that the educational sector should be restructured to achieve this goal. All levels of education should be restructured toward skills acquisition up to intermediate and tertiary stages.

It is consequently necessary that the right of the citizen to functional education should be enshrined in statue books as a fundamental right, to make it mandatory for the government to fund it.

Nelson Mandela was only stating the obvious when he observed that education was the most powerful weapon to change the world. However, for African countries, which need development, education of the citizenry must have the additional target of making them skilful. It is not enough to just produce graduates at different levels who are generally knowledgeable in the arts, the social sciences or sciences, without any particular skill to show for it. This will require an entire overhaul of the education curriculum. African education curriculum should be more technology-focused than just general knowledge oriented. Many African youths graduate at university level without learning anything about the technological inventions and breakthroughs in Egypt many centuries before Western technology saw the light. That is a shame.

African education curriculum must be carefully tailored to ensure that the early African technological feats are visited as a way of raising technological consciousness in the youths. This will equally fire them to think of technological innovations and prepare them better for skill acquisition.

Without education, there can hardly be development. Without technological inventors, there can hardly be industrialization. The education that African countries need is that which can fast-tack technological breakthroughs and industrialization. Any investment in this direction is worthwhile and should be encouraged. The logical thing for African countries, desirous of home-grown industrialization, to do is to make education, which must be functional and skill-acquisition driven, free and compulsory at all levels.

Right to Employment

When citizens right to gainful employment is enshrined in law. This is necessary for several reasons. When it is a right for every citizen, of working age, to have employment by law, the government will see employment generation as an important responsibility. This will compel the government to enable the growth of the private sector and create jobs. The basic assumption here is that every citizen of working age has one competitive skill or the other, resulting from an already established education order which ensures free, compulsory and functional education at all levels for all citizens. This being so, when the government fails in her responsibility to provide gainful employment to a citizen, the affected person can enforce his right and compel the government to either provide him with a job or pay him compensation. The logical expectation in the circumstance, is that the government will make unemployment benefits available to the unemployed to avoid litigation. Again, in order not to expend huge amounts of money on payment of unemployment claims, the government will expectedly intensify efforts at promoting job creation policies.

The African situation needs something uncommon to stimulate productivity and industrialization. A polity that focuses on getting people to work and arming them with requisite skills will, no doubt, help in this direction. The more people skilled to work are at work, the better for the productive capacity of each nation. And the more the productive capacity, the greater the chances of industrialization. When citizens have the right to gainful employment enshrined in law as an economic right, those who govern will have to implement the law, which in turn will energize productivity and industrialization.

Right to Good Health Service

It is only a healthy citizenry that can be productive. A sick citizenry will be too weak to produce anything.

In Africa, a lot of preventable and curable diseases claim many lives because health facilities and medication are not available and the people are too poor to access and afford available ones. Many Africans die every day because healthcare services are too expensive or simply unavailable.

The greater threat to Africa's development is the poor health conditions of her citizenry. Like the saying goes, health is wealth, and naturally, a continent where a majority of citizens are sick and dying cannot equate to wealth. To say that the poor health status of Africans is a major evidence of their poverty is to state the obvious.

The right to good health must consequently be seen as an economic right, for as already noted, there can be no productivity in bad health. Citizens need to be healthy to create wealth by engaging in production. Consequently, the right to good health service must be legally guaranteed as an economic right.

This will entail mandatory provision of health insurance cover by all levels of government in collaboration with all employers of labour. In addition, the government should ensure that healthcare delivery is within reach of every segment of the population. The private sector should be compelled to have a functional health clinic for its staff. The bottom line is that good health as the economic right of the citizen, will require that affordable and quality healthcare delivery be available, and all citizens who have reason to believe that this right was denied them can seek legal redress.

To fund affordable healthcare for the citizenry, a National Health Care Delivery Fund (NHCDF), should be established. All tiers of government shall be compelled by law to contribute two percent (2%) of their monthly earnings to the fund. In like manner, all major Corporate Organisations making up to $5m (Five million dollars) annual profit will be compelled by law to contribute one percent (1%) of their pre-tax profit to the fund. In addition, there should be a 1% (one percent) Health Service Tax (HST) charged on every consumable luxury service, such as alcohol, cigarettes, restaurants, hotel bills, cinemas, and sundry others. This tax will be paid into the NHCDF.

The fund will be managed by a National Health Care Delivery Commission (NHCDC). This Commission will be duplicated at the state and local levels. Each month the commissions shall meet to allocate the funds to all of its three tiers at the ratio of 30% for National, 30% for State and 40% for local commissions. With ready funds, each commission will be compelled by law, to use the funds to attend to the healthcare needs of the people, as articulated by the different levels of the economic councils (details on the councils are contained in subsequent chapters) relevant to the levels of government, that is, National, State and Local.

Why is There Emphasis on Economic Rights?

Econocracy places emphasis on economic rights over other rights because it is practically impossible for an impoverished citizen to enforce his political, social or liberal rights.

These rights which are generally referred to as human rights in liberal democracies or civil liberties are basically expressions of aspects of man's freedom or rights that must be protected by law, and should not be abused by the State. They include freedom of speech, freedom of expression, freedom of association and freedom of worship. There is also the right to life, equality before the law or what is commonly referred to as the rule of law.

However, before a citizen can enforce or enjoy any of these rights, he must be economically viable. A poor, uneducated citizen is already encumbered by his economic status and can hardly enjoy or enforce any of these rights. How does one freely express himself when he is uneducated? Education liberates the mind and emboldens it with the self-confidence needed for self-expression in a confident and purposeful manner. In the first place, the right to freedom of expression presupposes that the individual exercising such right is sufficiently informed on issues of public interest. It is public awareness that makes him join in a public debate.

What is there to freely express other than to join issues on matters of public concern such as good governance, public sector accountability and preservation of the dignity of man? For an individual to effectively and confidently contribute in such public debates, he or she will require an understanding of the issues at stake. To understand the issue at stake will require sufficient education. Without education, a citizen is shut out from informed public and private debates and therefore is unable to exercise their rights of freedom of expression. In such a situation, only the educated and economically viable partake in public debates on the well-being of their nations.

In Africa, where literacy level is low, the implication is that only a minority exercise these rights. These few people are the ones that determine how the country is governed. By implication, what is in place in Africa is the rule by a few (aristocracy). To reverse this will require the right to free, compulsory, functional education at all levels. It is only by so doing that more people will be educated and therefore be in a position to express their right to freedom of speech or expression.

The same can be said about the right of freedom of association. Citizens require a certain level of confidence to exercise this freedom. In the wake of the election of Donald Trump as the president of the United States in November 2016 and his inauguration in January 2017, hundreds of Americans took to the streets in different states of the US to protest and raise alarm over their perceptions of the direction of his presidency. They did not need any permit to exercise their right to freedom of association. They were in the streets for days until they called off the protests themselves.

In contrast, similar protests were to be staged in Nigeria in January 2017 by some concerned citizens to protest the worsening economic conditions in the country. The police said they did not have permit to protest and did everything to thwart the plan. In the end, the protest was held, albeit completely whittled down, amidst heavy police presence. Many who would have ordinarily participated in the protest backed out because they feared that violent clashes with the police would trail the protest, which could result in casualties as had happened in the past.

The US example is typical with most Western democracies' freedom of association, including the freedom to protest which is virtually unhindered in these countries, as we see often in United Kingdom,

Germany, France, etc. The opposite is the case in Africa. The Nigerian example is not peculiar to Nigeria. It is the same story in Zimbabwe, Rwanda, Gambia, Egypt, and virtually all African countries.

The only factor that explains the difference is the fact that most of the citizens of the West are educated, gainfully employed and therefore confident enough to assert their right to freedom of association. Their African counterparts are mostly uneducated, impoverished and sick. They are largely lethargic and unable to assert their rights. They are easily intimidated by State power and in the process they become too timid to make any impact or to enforce any rights.

Economic determination of human rights is more pronounced on the issue of equality before the law or rule of law. The technicalities of Western legal system make litigation and the legal process expensive for any individual to effectively enforce his legally guaranteed rights. The services of a legal practitioner, who must be paid necessary fees, is usually required. Many Africans are either unemployed, under employed or unemployable and can hardly make ends meet. They can ill-afford the payment of such legal fees. The wretched, unemployed majority cannot even tinker with the prospect of any form of litigation. Their daily preoccupation is how to find the next meal. The result is that most of them willingly surrender their rights for lack of means to enforce them. How can there be equality before the law in such a situation? It is common knowledge that justice in most African countries is at the beck and call of the few wealthy people. Most of the African citizenry, who belong to what Fanon refers to as the "wretched of the earth," are not even looking forward to any justice from the labyrinth of the Western legal system that defines the functions of the law in their nations.

When we look at it from the aspect of the rule of law, the same scenario of the rich having advantage over the poor applies. As I pointed out in my book, "Election Finance and Corruption in Nigeria: An Investment Theory Approach," the relevant electoral laws that require that those who run elections for President, Governor, National Assembly, etc., publicly declare and account for their sources of election funds, have been breached by politicians. These laws state that politicians who flout them should be tried, and upon conviction, be liable to a fine or imprisonment. So far, no politician has been arraigned nor tried for breaking these laws. The other side of the coin is that the poor illiterate street vendor, who violates city edicts and hawks fruits or similar goods in Abuja or Lagos, is constantly harassed and arrested. People are arrested every day for breaking traffic rules and many other civil offences. If the rule of law actually rules in Nigeria, many politicians would have been arrested and tried for not complying with relevant electoral laws on election finance. That is just one instance. Many other examples abound. Again, the situation in Nigeria is no different from the situation in most African countries.

At play here is the power of wealth or economic well-being. The wealthy and influential can conveniently ignore or break the law and nothing happens, but the poor pays for any law they break. Can it be said then that the law rules? The concept of the rule of law is that nobody is above the law. Everybody is subject to the law. Why does this seem to work in the West and not in Africa? The same reason that I adduced earlier still applies.

A greater percentage of the citizenry of Western countries are educated, employed and self-confident. Because of their level of sophistication, they will expose and challenge whosoever breaks the law, no matter how highly placed, including the President or Prime Minister. As a result, what I will call "societal alert" on compliance with the rule of law, particularly among public office holders, becomes a norm.

Everyone, including the public office holder, is conscious of the fact that the man next door is watching him very closely and will expose any arrogation of the law unto himself. That consciousness keeps everyone in check, and makes the enforcement of the rule of law feasible.

Expectedly, the reverse is the case in Africa. The poor, unemployed majority have been intimidated into psychological surrender. In the actual sense of it, they see those in public office as demigods who either fought or bought their way to power. They, on the other hand, are too weak and timid to query public officials for abuse of power or outright flouting of the law. For their own safety, they prefer to keep mute if and when they stumble upon incriminating evidence that the high and mighty in public office is lawless. Worst of all, they believe they have no stake and should be less bothered by what happens in the colony of the rich and powerful. That is the irony of the African situation which makes the rule of law, an importation from liberal democratic tradition, a mere ornament on the statute books. It is clear that truly, economic superstructure should determine the political structure. It is only when economic rights have been secured that the rights to shelter, functional education, employment, and good health must be seen as economic rights. They are rights that liberate man from the shackles of poverty, low self-esteem, sickness, and self-subordination. Without this economic liberation, political rights in Africa will remain a mirage for the poor and oppressed.

My position is that in Africa, economics should define politics not the other way round. If you allow politics to define economics in Africa, politics will approach economics in a Western imperialist coloration of trying to secure human rights before economic rights. What should be said at this point is that citizens of the West secured their economic rights through various revolutions across history. Several of these revolutions were against monarchy by their subjects, against capital by labour, and against dictatorship by democratic activism.

The enactment of human rights as the rights of citizens was like the crowning glory to these struggles. Unfortunately for Africa, colonialism conquered her and subjected her to a state of docility by sheer brute force. In a way, although Africa did not benefit from the revolutions of the West, she was forced to accept its high points: the attainment of civic rights as a take-off point. This amounts to doing the last thing first and needless to add that it can hardly work. The solution lies in the realization that while a revolutionary road might not be imperative, economic liberation through the enforcement of economic rights will serve the same purpose.

This is what Econocracy is all about. It hopes to achieve for Africa, in a peaceful ordered manner, what the revolutions achieved for the West. Let me add that we have only tried to define Econocracy. In the course of the book, I shall outline how it will work, determine politics and ensure accelerated development for Africa.

Our next chapter will examine why liberal democracy cannot guarantee development in Africa.

Chapter 3

LIBERALISM AS EPOCH IN WESTERN EVOLUTION

The Age of Enlightenment in Europe, also known as the Age of Reason, was epoch in the historical dialectics of the continent. It was an intellectual movement that dominated Europe during the 18th century. Its main thrust was the fiery postulation that civil actions should be propelled by reason. It also advanced the paradigm that reason should be the primary source of authority and the legitimacy of government.

The intellectuals or philosophers who pioneered this extraordinary epoch advanced such ideas as liberty, constitutional government, separation of religion from state, tolerance, and opposition to the monocracy. Before then, the monarchy was seen as a divine enactment, implying that monarchs had divine right to rule, otherwise known as divine right of kings. This intellectual challenge of the divine right of kings was so fundamental and impactful, that it made much difference in the nation of subsequent European governments. To this extent, it can be said that the Age of Enlightenment was the defining era in Europe's march towards liberal democracy. It was during this period that European thinkers laid the foundation for the many revolutions that rocked and changed Europe's political landscape by replacing monarchical rule with the rule of the people through representatives.

The commencement of the Age of Enlightenment is traced from the death of Louis XIV in 1715 to the final outbreak of the French Revolution of 1789. The scientific revolution of the 1620s in Europe can be said to be the forerunner of the Enlightenment Age.

However, the epochal transformation that the age brought to Europe, was the challenge to the authority of the monarchy and the church, that paved the way for the political revolutions of the 18th and 19th centuries. This was the era that ushered in liberal democracy (henceforth liberalism), to Europe and North America. It was a process that gave birth to a product, a phenomenon, not one magic wand that dropped from the moon. It was a response to the challenges of the people at that time, namely the absolute rule of the monarchy and the all-pervasive influence of the church at the time. Liberalism is therefore not the end of the quest for a better political ideology for governance, as African leaders seem to believe.

A more vivid description of this era is provided by (Makherjee & Ramaswamy, 2007) in which they described the Enlightenment Age as "the liberation of man from self-imposed tutelage. Tutelage is the incapacity of using one's own understanding except under the direction of another. This tutelage is self-imposed when its cause lies not in the lack of understanding but in a lack of resolution and of courage. Dare to use your own understanding. That is the motto of enlightenment. Self-thinking was to seek the highest touchstone of truth in oneself, i.e., one's own reason."

The two scholars went further to say that *"the basic idea underlying all the tendencies of enlightenment was the conviction that human understanding is capable, by its own power and without any recourse to supernatural assistance, of comprehending the system of the world and that this new way of understanding the world will lead to a new way of mastering it."* As can be seen from the description of the Age of Enlightenment, it is all about man's reliance on human reason to conquer his environment. It is like a challenge to humanity to wake up and come to grips with the reality that it has the reasoning capacity to free itself from a self-imposed tutelage of the monarchy or aristocracy and from absolute rule or dictatorship. It is a reassurance that man has the capacity to assert himself and be truly free to enjoy his inalienable God-given rights.

These new ideas were formulated by such notable

philosophers as Voltaire, Jean-Jacques Rousseau, Montesquieu, Adam Smith, Jeremy Bentham, and Immanuel Kant, amongst others.

However, earlier philosophers such as Francis Bacon and John Locke, are believed to have influenced them. They spread their enlightenment gospel through thought-provoking publications. Such publications include (Voltaire, Letters on the English, 1733) and (Voltaire, Philosophical Dictionary, 1764), (Rousseau J. J., 1754), (Rousseau J. J., 1762), (Smith, 1776) and (Montesquieu, 1748).

John Locke's ideas influenced 18th century French society a great ideal. (Mbachu, 1998) argues that Locke's name dominated 18th century France, stressing that his essay concerning human understanding spotlighted experience as the sole source of knowledge. He was opposed to a scheme of life that emphasized authority rather than reason and observation. According to Mbachu, *"Locke's two treaties of government and letters concerning toleration showed the outline of a new social order in which despotic kingship by divine right and clerical control of thought and education in religion, were replaced by political liberalism and intellectual individualism."*

Political liberalism and intellectual individualism can be summed as the driving force that shaped the 18th century Enlightenment Age in Europe. Most of the thinkers of that era reflected this broad focus in their writing. For instance, Voltaire, an 18th century French Enlightenment thinker, after spending some time in England, wrote his French letters which was aimed at exposing to the whole of Europe, a new political and social order in England worthy of emulation.

Mbachu (1998, 18), recalls that Voltaire, after spending three years in England, from 1726, wrote his Letters on the English, which "showed the French and Europe reading public a land of freedom and common sense, secular in outlook, tolerant in religion and respect of law." He further noted that Voltaire was favourably impressed with the rising social prestige of the middle classes in England and with the individual freedom that resulted from wealth earned in trade and commerce.

On the other hand, Montesquieu was famous for his work on the Spirit of the Laws. He too travelled to England and thereafter acknowledged the sound common sense of the English leadership as well as flowering free press. He admired England as a nation passionately fond of liberty. He advocated faith in human progress through reason. He believed that human reason should try and decipher the spirit of the law which he sees as more important than the land itself. As Mbachu (1998, 93) observed, Montesquieu believed the laws *"should be relative to the climate of each country, to the quality of its soil, to its situation and extent to the principal occupation of the nations."* He believed that the origin of the English political life can be traced to the remote history of the people rather than the charter of the constitution. This means that the government of a people is a product of their evolutionary process. These evolutionary process for Montesquieu, are a combination of physical and environmental factors on the one hand, and of psychological motivations on the other.

However, Montesquieu's most outstanding contribution to the Age of Enlightenment is his doctrine of separation of powers through which he sought a balanced constitution in which executive and legislative powers should be separate and vested on different bodies.

Montesquieu was impressed with the English system which he saw as favouring individual liberty, property and ancient privilege of aristocracy. Mbachu (1998, 96), notes that although the forms of state – monarchy, aristocracy and democracy – were united in English government, the powers of government were separated from one another, leading Montesquieu to believe that "there can be no liberty where the executive legislative and judicial powers are united in one person or body of persons because such concentration is bound to result to arbitrary despotism."

It is a known fact that Montesquieu's ideas were shared by the framers of the American constitution, who fully applied the doctrine of separation of powers, resulting in the exclusion of cabinet ministries from the legislative arm of government.

(Ferguson J. , 1994) noted that Benjamin Franklin visited Europe repeatedly at the period of the Enlightenment and contributed actively to the scientific and political debates there and brought back some of the ideas to Philadelphia. He also recalled that Thomas Jefferson closely followed the Enlightenment ideas and later incorporated some of the ideas of the Enlightenment into the United States Declaration of Independence (1776), while others, like James Madison, incorporated them into the constitution in 1787.

According to Mukherjee and Ramaswamy (2007, 213), Jean-Jacques Rousseau (1712 – 1778) was the greatest that the French produced during this era. They believe that in the entire history of political theory, he was the most exciting and most provocative.

These scholars, quoting Heavashaw (1931), summarized the enduring philosophical attribution of Rousseau's social and political ideas as *"firstly, the idea that people are the ultimate source of all legitimate territorial authority; secondly, that government is merely the agent and delegate of the sovereign people; thirdly, that the common good is the criterion of social legislation and satisfactory administration; fourthly, that the state is organic in nature and not a mere mechanism; fifthly, that the true basis of political obligation is consent hence, finally, that there is in the last resort no antagonism between freedom and authority, law and liberty, man and the State."*

(Rousseau J. J., 1762), Rousseau's thoughts are mostly expressed in his second book, The Social Contract, which was by far more popular than his first book, Emile, which spelt out a new education system that can produce an undertreated natural man. The Social Contract however distinguished him as an outstanding thinker and philosopher. His concern in the book was to formulate an association which shall have the capacity to defend the common good and in which man will unite himself with all for the defence of the common good, even while he remains as free as he originally was. Rousseau appears to have been greatly motivated by the need for a *"Social Contract"*; (Cranston, 1979) observed that this desire was expressly stated at the beginning of his book when he lamented that "man is born free and everywhere he is in chains."

The summary of Rousseau's *The Social Contract* is that there is a need for man to live in a more secure environment, by associating himself to a collective sovereign of an entire society or territorial political expression and combine same with his individual liberty which he had before joining the association.

As Mukherjee and Ramaswamy (2007, 213) put it,

"Rousseau's sovereign is the externalized general will, and, as has been said before, stands essentially the same as the natural harmonious order. In marrying the concept with the principle of popular sovereignty and popular self-expression, Rousseau gave rise to the totalitarian democracy."

Another of the Enlightenment thinkers, Immanuel Kant (1724 – 1804), equally harped on individual freedom and political authority. He tried to reconcile rationalism and religious belief by mapping out a roadmap for a public that will be governed by private and public reason.

Bentham was famous for his doctrine of utilitarianism. He espoused this in his work, (Bentham, 1789). He was concerned with ensuring the personal happiness of the individual, alongside the happiness of the greatest number of people. This appears contradictory because often times, individual happiness may not agree with the happiness of the greater number of people. An individual's happiness may be selfishly motivated, thus at variance with that of others which may not be no less selfishly motivated.

Bentham, however, proffers a way out of this dilemma by proposing two means through which the inherit contradiction between individual selfishness and communal good can be averted, which is through education. Bentham consequently proposed a system of public education because, through education, man's mind can be elevated to understand that rationally-conceived happiness of one's self includes goodwill, sympathy and benevolence for others (Mbachu 1998, 118). The second proposal by Bentham, Mbachu points out, is the creation of an institutional environment in which man's selfish impulse can be channelled into socially useful purpose so that it will be contrary to his self-interest to harm others.

The purpose here is to draw attention to the thought pattern that characterized the Age of Enlightenment in Europe, to sharpen our understanding of how the age influenced the emergence of liberal democracy in the West. The few examples above serve this purpose. We have seen that the dominant theme of that era was the need to preserve individual freedom and secure the State from the tyranny of the monarchy and the undue influence of the Church.

These ideas were so powerful that they truly influenced the state of political affairs in Europe and America. Indeed, the concept of liberal democracy is traceable to this age.

Specifically, the ideas of the enlightenment directly influenced the French and American revolutions. In general, reforms and revolutions, following the overwhelming influence of the Age of Enlightenment, helped to move European countries towards liberal democracy.

Evidence abound all through European history, that the above assertion is correct. In Portugal, the Marquis of Pombal, who was the head of government then, implemented comprehensive socio-economic reforms reflective of the sentiments of the Enlightenment Age. The government abolished slavery, introduced secular public schools, significantly weakened the Inquisition and restructured the tax system. All these put together, gave Portugal's government a progressive outlook even while she remained under a powerful dictator.

There are also historical reports that other European leaders welcomed Enlightenment protagonists to their court and actually requested them to help them formulate laws and programs that would enable them reform their countries and build stronger, less vulnerable states. Historians record that among the European leaders who took such bold steps were Fredrick the Great of Prussia, Catherine the Great of Russia, Leopard II of Tuscany, and Joseph II of Austria. The evidence that they bought into the enlightenment doctrine can be seen from the fact that they were known thereafter as enlightenment depots.

Fredrick the Great actually went out of his way to identify with the Enlightenment Age. He openly fraternized with

Enlightenment thinkers, philosophers and scientists at his court. One such instance was his invitation to Voltaire to live in his palace, which the later eagerly accepted. At that time, Voltaire had just finished serving a prison sentence by the French authorities, where he was badly maltreated. Nothing can attest better to the influence the enlightenment had on Fredrick than his public declaration that his principal occupation was *"to combat ignorance and prejudice, to enlighten minds, cultivate morality, and to make people as happy as it suits human nature and at the means as my disposal permit."*

In both Portugal and Denmark, their leaders also governed according to Enlightenment ideas, the same goes for Poland, whose model constitution of 1791 clearly expressed enlightenment ideas.

However, even as the European mornachies and aristocracies laboured to embrace and implement Enlightenment reforms, the public did not show equal excitement. The citizenry, having been soaked in the idea of individual liberty and freedom, and free from the stranglehold of the monarchy and religion, did not appear sufficiently impressed with these reforms, which they did not see as going far enough. They remained unshaken in their newfound ideas on how best state authority must be deployed to ensure the happiness for the greatest number of people under a truly free and liberal arrangement.

A typical example is Austria where Joseph was so enthusiastic about reforms that he actually rolled out as many reform programmes as he could conjecture. In spite of his enthusiasm, the public remained unimpressed. Revolts broke out and virtually all his programmes were torpedoed by the public.

No doubt, the Enlightenment Age had a more profound impact on Europe through the French revolution of 1789, which was also fuelled by the American revolution of 1776. Historians such as Giles Macdonough pointedly linked the Enlightenment Age to the French Revolutions (MacDonogh, 1999). The major political change that the Enlightenment brought to Europe was a paradigm shift in the conception of government from the concept of the divine right of kings to that of a system legitimized only through individual liberty guaranteed by the liberal democratic ideas. To this extent, it can be said that the European revolutions of the late 1700s and early 1800s were caused by the fact that this governance paradigm shift could not be implemented through a peaceful means but through violent revolutions. This was essentially because the new idea of enlightenment that citizens, by natural law, must consent to the acts and rulings of their government was in direct conflict with the one that existed hitherto where the king was never wrong as his rule was ordained by God.

According to Alexis De Tocqueville, (Tocqueville, 1856), the French Revolution was the inevitable result of the radical opposition created in the 18th century between the monarchy and the men of letters of Enlightenment. His view is that "these men of letters constituted a sort of substitute aristocracy that was both all-powerful and without real power. This illusory power came from the rise of public opinion, born when absolutist centralization removed the nobility and the bourgeois from the political sphere."

De Tocqueville concludes that the literary politics that resulted promoted a discourse of equity and was consequently in fundamental opposition to the monarchical regime.

It is clear from all the foregoing, that the Age of Enlightenment did not just redefine politics in Europe and America and the rest of the West, but fostered liberalism as the consequence of its influence. The point of interest to us here is that because liberalism sprang from the idea of the Enlightenment Age in Europe, it must be seen as a reaction to the political conditions of the people at that time. Again, because the people themselves bought into the Enlightenment Age, which did not just capture the oppressive socio-political conditions they suffered, but in addition, proffered a way forward, they were prepared to take the necessary steps to enforce those ideas. Those necessary steps were inevitably revolutionary and violent. Noteworthy also, is the fact that the people, having secured their own system of government (liberalism), by themselves through themselves, remained eternally vigilant in the protection of that system over the ages. Also, the political class that emerged from this process, knowing how and why they emerged, remained conscious of the need not to fall back to any form of dictatorial tendencies that could remind the citizenry of the monarchical era and consequently trigger a new set of revolutions that could consume them. This eagle-eyed vigilance of the citizenry and the alertness of the political class against slipping back to totalitarianism in the use of political power, are the twin checks that keep liberalism alive in Western democracies. As we shall find out in the next chapter, they are also the factors that have defined development in the West and ensured that they remain developed. After all, individual liberty and freedom will amount to naught without economic prosperity and better living standards.

It should be obvious that the opposite will naturally be the effect when liberalism is adopted and applied undiluted, by societies that did not exactly pass through the European evolutionary process. As Adam Ferguson will argue, politics grows out of social developments, which I prefer to refer to, as the evolutionary process.

In his book, (Ferguson A. , 1767), submits that there are four stages in this social development which he used to explain how man advances from the stages of a hunting and gathering society, to a commercial and civil society without signing a contract.

The problem with applying political panacea groomed and cultured by another clime as in the case of liberalism, to a continent such as Africa, which was not part of the evolutionary process, is that the borrowers can mistake the fine aroma of the doctrine, to represent a magic wand that can catapult them from poverty or backwardness to development. As I noted earlier, liberalism offers an attractive political aroma indeed. With provisions such as free, fair elections, freedom of speech and association, and a long list of other freedoms and rights, undiscerning nations may be quick to embrace it as a solution to their political and economic development problems. However, this is far from correct. The two main ingredients identified earlier as the mainstay of liberalism, that is, the vigilance of the citizenry and the alertness of the political leadership, will be lacking in such societies which will make success elusive.

Besides, as I hinted earlier, a top-to-bottom approach will amount to truncating the natural law of social evolution or what Ferguson calls the four stages of social progress. We may liken this natural law to the development of humans from childhood to adulthood. As we shall see, there is a natural, divinely ordered process through which a child must pass to reach adulthood. These stages are infancy, characterized by immobility, when the child cannot move from one point to another without assistance; later infancy, when the child begins to crawl; mid infancy, when the child is able to stand and walk and transit; then adulthood, when he can run, go on errands, from which stage he finally matures to manhood.

Should it not surprise us that despite all the wonders of science, such as the invention of the aeroplane, exploration of space, cloning and artificial insemination, it has not been possible to invent any device that can circumvent this natural progression of human beings from childhood to manhood?

The truth is that no feat of science has been able to make man skip any of the stages of progression to maturity by first crawling then attempting to walk, with all the attendant hazards, before finally walking, then running and much later being able to play the game of football.

The inability of almighty science to accomplish this feat will suggest that this is one natural (divine) order that is immutable. It appears inevitable to conclude that any attempt to short-change this order can only lead to a chaotic end. Let us imagine the consequences of trying to make a child to walk within the first seven days of its life by injecting it with some substance that can make it mature faster. Or imagine for that matter trying to make a three-month old baby play football by injecting it with maturity enhancing drugs. Such attempts will only end in disaster.

We must therefore accept that the same fate that awaits any attempt to change the natural order of the human progression to maturity awaits a society which tries to change its order of progression. If we can see society here as the macro version of the human being, moving from "a hunting and gathering society, to a commercial and civil society", then it should follow this natural order. Africa was at the hunting and gathering stage when colonialism assaulted her and took her captive, forcing her to swallow European values without being part of the process that produced such values. The forceful imposition of liberalism on Africa was one such assault. At independence, Africans were left with the two alternatives of either choosing the presidential or parliamentary systems of governments, or the federal or unitary political unions, because they were the only ones that liberalism offered.

The catastrophic consequences is that while the West has continued to soar higher and higher in development because of their hard-earned liberal values, Africa has remained perennially unstable and has continued to politically and economically depend on the West. This was what Western liberalism set out to achieve in the first place. For over sixty years since many African countries secured independence from Europe, they have continued without success to try and apply liberal ideas to their development needs. The reason is not far-fetched: liberalism is not home grown. African political ideology and Africans are strangers to the long and bloody road that the European people walked to reach this ideology.

Because of this, the conditions precedent for the effective workings of liberalism, such as enlightened citizenry, high literacy level, and an independent and critical media, which are present in the West, are absent in Africa. In the absence of these social forces, it is difficult for liberalism to truly flourish in our societies. Subsequent chapters of this book will provide more details on this by showing how and why liberalism works in the West, and has stimulated economic growth and political stability, while in Africa, it has become the major factor that has continued to under-develop the continent. Thus far, I have tried to create an understanding of what liberalism stands for, because I intend to use the ideology which applies to both the West and Africa to show why Europe stays developed while Africa has remained the opposite.

Chapter 4

WHY LIBERALISM DEVELOPED THE WEST

We have already identified two key factors that sustain liberalism in the West: the eternal vigilance of the populace and the no less eternal alertness of the political leadership. These two core factors, in their expanded forms, account for the success of liberalism as a tool for the development of the West, specifically Europe and North America. Eternal vigilance ensures that the populace defend their democratically guaranteed rights otherwise known as the fundamental human rights. Coming from the age of letters, otherwise known as the Enlightenment Age, as we have seen, the populace also acquired the literacy culture which encouraged them to use literacy means to express and defend their rights. A major outcome of this is the free, independent and critical media – as we have them today in the West, a sine qua non for the sustenance of liberal democracy. On the other hand, the alertness of the political leadership ensures that they are ever willing to submit themselves to the scrutiny of the people, thereby remaining accountable to them. At any rate, a critical media will always keep leaders on their toes and ensure that they are ever accountable to the people.

One of the major innovations of liberalism is regular elections, wherein the people elect representatives to lead them for a period of time. This is best appreciated when considered against the background of perpetual rule of the monarchy, where the European countries came from, as already noted in previous chapters, the monarchy with its claim of divine right to rule and its replacement with elected representative of the people. Part of the measures adopted by the people to ensure that no one ever had the opportunity to perpetuate himself in power was through the adoption of the periodic election process. The duration from 4 – 7 years, from country to country, within which new elections must be held to either revalidate the political mandate given to political leaders by the people or issue a fresh one. The beauty of this process is that even in a parliamentary agreement that has no fixed tenure for leaders, they submit themselves to a validation of their mandate through elections, which must hold after a given period. In like manner, although legislatures in presidential systems of government may not have fixed tenures, they also must submit themselves to periodic elections to revalidate their mandate from the people.

However, the outcomes of these elections will not reflect the true wishes and aspirations of the people if they are not truly free and fair. Without the eternal vigilance of the people, politicians may actually try one way or another to thwart the electoral process and subvert the will of the people through election rigging, vote buying or other corrupt means. Besides, it is in the nature of man to try to cut corners, particularly in politics, effective institutional checks, backed by vigilant public can thwart this natural tendency. The instance of the Watergate scandal of 1964 and the Peerage scandal in the United Kingdom of 1923 clearly vindicate this position. In the Watergate scandal, President Richard Nixon tried to use unorthodox means to gain electoral advantage for his Republican party by secretly tapping the headquarters of the Democratic party. In the Peerage scandal of the United Kingdom, politicians sold Peerage to the people for political gains that would give them electoral edge in general elections. The vigilance of the people and the watchdog role of a critical media truncated these illegal moves. Simply put, a vigilant populace and a critical media are inevitable precondition for the success of liberal democracy.

However, for the public to play the roles effectively, they must be reasonably knowledgeable and politically active. The first leads to the second. A knowledgeable populace will invariably be politically involved and active. Conversely, an ignorant populace will invariably be politically docile. The populace in Europe is highly knowledgeable and therefore politically active. The Enlightenment philosophy mostly pontificated through several publications and books, as we saw earlier, can only be appreciated by a literate, knowledgeable populace. This was why the Enlightenment had impact leading to the many violent revolutions that toppled the monarchies and aristocracies. The West had demonstrated this level of awareness through knowledge, particularly since the Age of Enlightenment.

After independence in 1776, a British parliamentary committee that visited the United States in 1780s was quite impressed with the mass education policy that the committee members, Joseph Whitwort and George Wallis observed: "Everybody reads... and intelligence penetrates through the lower grades of society." Most states had compulsory education laws requiring a minimum of three months per year schooling for child factory workers. It is when almost everybody reads that a literary culture can be sustained. In the West, that culture has been entrenched for a long time. It is much easier also to sustain a literary culture in a society that has a common language. Information dissemination will be much easier because most of the people will be able to read the information so circulated. Virtually Western European and North American societies have one language. The United Kingdom

(English), Germany (German), France (French), Belgium (Dutch, French and German), Holland (Dutch), Netherlands (Dutch), Portugal (Portuguese), Austria (German), Switzerland (Swiss), United States (English), Canada (English/French), Italy (Italian). With a common language, it is easier to disseminate knowledge and to breed an educated populace. The literacy level in Western Europe and the United States and Canada clearly confirm that a sustained knowledgeable populace has been in place from the Age of Enlightenment to date; virtually every citizen in these Western countries can read and write. It is because the citizens in the West are knowledgeable that they are equally active politically.

Both before and after the election and inauguration of Donald Trump as the 45th President of the United States, many Americans resorted to street protest to register their anger over their perceptions that President Trump may operate in a manner that may threaten or trample on their fundamental rights. The protest lasted for days across many States of the US.

At the point in question, Trump had not taken any presidential action that was inimical to the preservation of the rights of the people. The mere perception that he could, sparked off the protest. The protest was therefore more like warning shot than a reaction to any action.

It was like the people were telling Trump, "Don't try us or you will regret it." This is not just political activism but a very proactive one at that. If mere perception could induce such mass protests that lasted for days, it is left to be imagined what the people will do when a concrete action has been taken by a president which they see as undermining their rights. The fact that these rights were secured on the bloody altars of revolution across Western Europe and America always serve as constant reminders to leaders that if the need arises, the people can revert to the same road they had travelled before and re-assert their rights. The anti-Trump protest in early 2017 just cited the point clearly of the eternal vigilance of the people in this regard.

The vigilance of the people is made more durable and effective through an independent and critical media. The perception of Donald Trump, by the American people who took to the streets in January 2017, was informed by what they heard and saw from the media before and after the elections. Because the media was free and independent, it reported everything said and done by Trump in his capacity as presidential candidate, President-elect and President. Some members of the public interpreted some of the things he said and did to suggest that he could be embarking on actions that could breed hate or discrimination on the basis of race or religion, which will be contrary to the provisions of the constitution of the US. Trump was so irked by the media coverage that he resorted to calling them names. This is about all he can do in the face of a critical media, because even as the President of the United States, he cannot abridge or attempt to tamper with the freedom of the press and freedom of speech clearly guaranteed in the American constitution. A US president is very unlikely to contemplate abridging the constitutionally guaranteed freedom of the press and/or the individual freedom of expression, because the inevitable public backlash can generate a hurricane strong enough to sweep any President away from the White House.

Again, the public backlash can only be unleashed by a politically knowledgeable and active populace.

The next logical link to a knowledgeable populace is that the political leadership is forced to remain accountable to them. Accountability here means that elected officials fulfil their campaign promises. They must also shun corruption and all corruptible influences, particularly those that can distract them from focusing on the implementation of their programme for the people. Because the people are politically aware and active, accountability of the leadership will also involve voting out those who fail to implement their campaign programmes. The logical thing to do for leaders towards re-election is to be faithful to the people and religiously implement the programme of their political parties as espoused by them in their election campaigns. This is a clear way to look at accountability by leaders because it goes to ensure that the people receive the fruits expected from the government being accountable to the people, which is an improvement in living standards. According to (Fukuyama, 1992), an accountable government means that the rulers believe that they are responsible to the people they govern and consequently put the people's interest above their own. He went further to explain, in what he describes as formal accountability (as it obtains in liberal democracies), that, "the government agrees to submit itself to certain mechanisms that limits its powers to do as it pleases." Ultimately, these procedures (which are usually spelt out in the constitution), allow the citizens of the society to replace the government entirely for malfeasance, incompetence, or abuse of power. Today, the dominant form of procedural accountability is elections, perfectly multi-party elections."

The citizens will gladly replace governments for incompetence, but a government that delivers on its programme will certainly be saved. This is the entire essence of the political programmes promised by politicians at campaigns. For the electorate therefore, the success or failure of any leader, set of leaders or government must be measured by how well those programmes impacted on the living standards of the people. Other sentiments could sometimes influence elections, but above every other factor is the well-being of the people. If the people adjudge from economic realities around them, that they were better off under a particular government, they are more likely to vote that government or candidate of the parties, back to power. If their judgement is the opposite, a reverse electoral verdict will most likely follow.

To this extent, it can be argued that the accountability of political leaders or government to the people, is measured by the impact their programme has on the wellbeing of the people. The effect of these programmes is referred to as development. When the programmes of government continuously and positively impact on the living standards of the people, it leads to overall development of the country. This explains why countries whose citizens have good living standards are said to be developed, while those that do not are said to be underdeveloped. Good living standards here, as we have also noted earlier, will be mirrored through available and affordable access to good healthcare delivery and the health status of the citizenry, employment, good housing, education and security of life and property. The more citizens have access to these provisions, the better their living standards. And the better the living standards of the citizenry, the more developed the society or country.

My position is that because of the historical antecedents

of liberal democracy in the West, the leaders are eternally at alert, conscious of the fact that they either remain accountable to the people or remain outside the precincts of governance. This consciousness ensures that they implement programmes that can create growth and development and therefore remain in government. This, among other factors, explains why and how liberalism has helped to develop Western countries.

There are ample evidences to show that the above assertion is correct. That is to say that the living standards of the citizenry in Western countries is good and that their countries are also developed. One way to measure this is through the Gross Domestic Product (GDP) and or Gross National Income (GNI) or Per Capita Income in these countries. Per capita income or average income actually measures the average income earned per person in a given country within specified period of one year.

Consequently, this may be the best way to measure the standard of living in any country because it is self-evident that the higher the income, the better the standard of living in a country. World Bank listing of per capita sovereign European countries which included eastern European countries for 2015, clearly show that Western European countries are in a better economic health than Eastern European countries.

Noteworthy, is that fact that while Western Europe was transferring from monarchy to popular rule, most of eastern Europe transited from monarchy to another totalitarian arrangement under socialism and communism. Eastern Europe merely moved from one totalitarian regime to another, which explains why they could not move at the same pace with their Western counterparts. This point is vividly driven home by (Acemoğlu & Robinson, 2012)) with their comparison of developments in North and South Korea after the Second World War in 1945. According to the scholars, the people of South Korea have living standards similar to those of Portugal and Spain, as against what is obtainable in North Korea, where living standards are akin to those of sub-Saharan African countries, which counts for about one-tenth of average living standards in South Korea. They pointed to the health of North Koreans, which, according to them, is in an even worse state, wherein the average North Korean can expect to live ten years less than his cousin in South Korea. The scholars went on to explain that the striking differences were not for any historical reasons, because they were not there before the end of the Second World War. They explained that in 1945, the different governments in the North and the South adopted very different ways of organizing their economies. South Korea adopted liberal democracy supported by the United States. North Korea opted for centralized community government, led by a few. Equally, South Korea had democratic institutions that included an open market economy, which allowed private investment and ownership of property, periodic election, and an accountable government. North Korea, on the other hand, was backed by the now defunct Soviet Union, to adopt a different approach to government which outlawed private ownership of property, introduced a centrally planned economy in what she called the "Juche System." Markets were closed and freedoms were curtailed and there were hardly free and fair elections. By the late 1990s, in just about half a century, South Korean growth and North Korean stagnation led to a tenfold gap between the two halves of this once-united country. The economic disaster of North Korea, which led to the starvation of millions, when placed against the South Korean economic success, is striking. Neither culture nor geography nor ignorance can explain the divergent paths of North and South Korea.

The North and South Korea examples can also explain why there is a difference in growth rate between East and West Europe. Under communism, the East adopted the centralized economic system which the now-defunct Soviet Union exported to North Korea. Since the breakup of the Soviet Union, most of the Eastern European countries have been eager to adopt open market economic policies. The difference in per capita income between the East and the West, as can be seen from Table 2, is still striking. Going by the statistics from the World Bank in 2015 as seen in the table, most East European countries fall within the upper middle-income range of $4,036 - $12,475 per capita and lower middle income of $1,026 - $4,035. This is in sharp contrast to all their Western European brothers who fall into the high-income brackets of $12,476 or more. In fact, the lowest per capita income from the table is Portugal $28,590, followed by Spain $34,490 and Italy $35,850. The rest of Western Europe has a per capita income of $40,000 above.

Table 2: *Per Capita Income of Western Europe. World Bank 2015 report.*

S/N	Country	Per Capita Income ($)
1	Austria	47,510
2	Belgium	40,840
3	Denmark	47,810
4	Finland	40,840
5	France	41,740
6	Germany	48,260
7	Iceland	46,120
8	Ireland	46,410
9	Italy	35,850
10	Luxemburg	70,750
11	Netherlands	48,400
12	Norway	64,590
13	Portugal	28,590
14	Spain	34,490
15	Sweden	47,390
16	Switzerland	61,930
17	United Kingdom	40,550

This is in sharp contrast to the picture in Eastern Europe where the country with the highest per capita is Slovenia – $30,840, followed by Czech Republic as seen in *table 3* below. The rest are $20,000 and below. There are countries with low records such as Moldavia, Ukraine, Georgia, and Kosovo.

Table 3: *Per Capita Income of Eastern Europe. World Bank 2015 report.*

S/N	Country	Per Capita Income ($)
1	Slovenia	30,840
2	Czech Republic	30,420
3	Slovakia	28,200
4	Estonia	27,510
5	Lithonia	26,660
6	Poland	25,400
7	Romania	24,600
8	Kazakhstan	24,260
9	Latvia	24,220
10	Russia	23,790
11	Moldavia	5,350
12	Ukraine	7,810
13	Georgia	9,410
14	Kosovo	9,840

Worthy of note also is the life expectancy profile of European countries. From the World Health Organization report for 2016 , all things being equal, as the economist will say, most Europeans expect to live up to 71 years at the maximum, but that applies to East European countries. In countries on the Western divide of Europe, the average citizen expects to remain alive until 80 years. This revelation is important, because it is a clear indication that healthcare delivery service in their countries is working and the citizens are quite healthy. The sharp contrast will be clear when we look at corresponding statistics on African countries in the next chapter.

Table 4 : *Life Expectancy of Europe (World Health Organisation) 2016*

Rank	Country	Life expectancy
1	Monaco	89.4
2	San Marino	83.4
3	Switzerland	83
4	Spain	82.8
5	Liechtenstein	82.7
6	Italy	82.7
7	Norway	82.5
8	Iceland	82.5
9	Luxembourg	82.3
10	France	82.3
11	Sweden	82.2
12	Malta	81.8
13	Finland	81.8

Rank	Country	Life expectancy
14	Ireland	81.6
15	Netherlands	81.5
16	Portugal	81.1
17	Greece	81
18	United Kingdom	81
19	Belgium	81
20	Austria	80.9
21	Slovenia	80.8
22	Denmark	80.7
23	Germany	80.6
24	Cyprus	80.5
25	Albania	78.3
26	Czech Republic	78.3
27	Croatia	78
28	Estonia	77.7
29	Poland	77.5
30	Montenegro	77.1
31	Bosnia and Herzegovina	76.9
32	Slovakia	76.6
33	Turkey	75.8
34	North Macedonia	75.7
35	Hungary	75.6
36	Serbia	75.2
37	Romania	75
38	Bulgaria	74.6
39	Latvia	74.5
40	Lithuania	74.3
41	Belarus	73.8
42	Ukraine	72.1
43	Moldova	71.6
44	Russia	71.6

The strong socio-political advantage that rubs off on developed countries through improved and better standards of living is that, with high income and good health at their disposal, their citizens become economically secure and socially confident. They can consequently further assert and defend their rights as citizens. Economic security naturally leads to self-confidence. A citizen who is less likely to worry about when his next meal will come, or how to attend to his health needs, is more likely to have the time and resources to defend and protest his rights, than the one who is hungry, poor, unhealthy and preoccupied with worries of how to meet these myriads of challenges.

As Francis Fukuyama (416) rightly observed, "Growth in per capita output does far more than out lager resources in the hands of States. It stimulates a broad transformation of society and mobilizes a host of new social forces that over time seek to become political actors as well."

The chain can be summarized this way: The Age of Enlightenment begat a knowledgeable populace leading to the emergence of independent critical media, condition which guarantees free and fair electoral process, that produces the framework of a State with strong institutions.

All these factors combined help to stimulate national development and economic prosperity (see *diagram 2*).

Diagram 2: *Framework of a State with Strong Institutions*

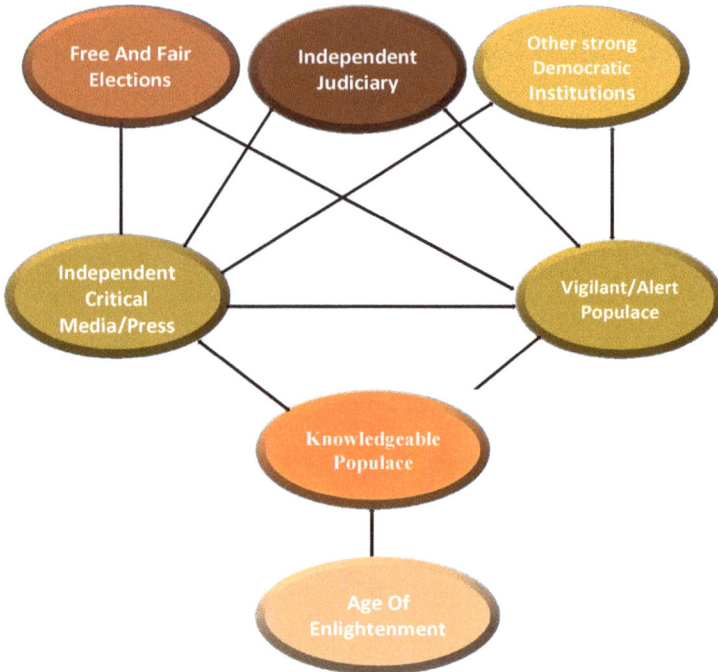

It will be impertinent to ignore the economic thrust of the liberal ideology we have tried to study in this chapter. It goes without saying that the soul of the liberalism is the enforcement of individual liberty against the stranglehold of despotic monarchs and the aristocrats, and liberty from centralized economic control. Under monarchical rule, central authority and government planning was the order of the day. This was a logical sequence to the doctrine of the divine right of kings in most of Europe at that time. The king could not be questioned because his authority came from God. This being so, how could anyone question that king's control of the economy? The control of trade, which was the major economic activity then, by the Crown was taken as given. Mercantilism was the order of the day and it allowed the Empire to maximize trade for the good of the Empire at the expense of rival empires. This was the dominant economic theory at that time. The advent of the Age of Enlightenment changed all that important intellectual argument in favour of a private system of ownership and the means of production, were eloquently advanced by a leading Enlightenment figure, John Locke. However, the credit for a complete redirection toward a market economy must be given to Adam Smith, who we met earlier as one of the Enlightenment philosophers.

Smith criticized mercantilism as ineffective in helping to grow the wealth of nations. His philosophy was profound in many ways. He was the first person to propose that the wealth of nations should not be measured in gold and silver but by the total of its production and commerce. This is known today as the Gross Domestic Product (GDP) which has become a scientific means of measuring a nation's wealth and development.

Before Smith, economists believed that a country's wealth was best measured by its store of gold and silver.

Smith also theorized that specialization of labour

will lead to greater productivity in the economy. But by far, the most profound of Smith's philosophy is his advancement of a free market economy which he says is most productive and beneficial to nations. He equally argued that the economic system of a nation should be based on individual self-interest led by an invisible hand, to achieve the greatest good for all.

There is little doubt about Smith's idea having far reaching influence on Western nations, as virtually all of them today operate free market economic systems, even if the degree varies from country to country. The coincidence of the publication of Smith's book in 1776, the same year America declared independence, may not exactly suggest his ideas had more impact on that country. Also, debates that followed the shaping of the American economy are quite suggestive of this.

The passage of the Poor Law Amendment Act in 1834 in the United States was against the economic philosophy that workers could be motivated by financial incentives. The Act limited the provision of social assistance to workers because of the belief in markets as the mechanism that can most effectively lead to wealth creation. The liberals who sponsored the passage of this Act also canvassed the position that individuals should be allowed to determine and secure their own economic self-interest without government direction or control.

By and large, the Age of Enlightenment helped to stimulate the growth of a free market economy in Europe, which can be said to be a facilitating hand in impressive economic development of Western nations. It appears that what Smith's ideas did to the West, Karl Max's did to the East. Max propagated the idea of centralized economic planning to enable workers control the means of production, otherwise known as socialism, which countries in the Eastern hemisphere embraced. A fierce rivalry of economic development models between the West and the East ensued shortly after the Second World War. This was generally known as the Cold War. The battle was between capitalism (open market economy) and socialism (centrally planned economy). So passionate was this ideological warfare that lesser countries who found themselves under the sphere of influence of any of these ideological divides were forced to adopt the ideology of the masters, whether it was the best for their situation or not. That was how North Korea and, until lately.

Countries like East Germany and Poland got stuck with socialism, while countries under the American sphere of influence had liberalism or capitalism forced down their throats. The sad thing in the African situation is that this Western pill has remained halfway in the throat, unable to go down fully and refusing to be thrown out. Our next chapter will examine why this development has kept Africa underdeveloped.

Chapter 5

HOW LIBERALISM FAILED AFRICA

Of the four components of liberalism, which we have been investigating as having the capacity to fuel the transformation of liberal democracies, as platforms for creating development and economic prosperity – knowledgeable populace, independent and critical media, free and fair elections, and strong state institutions – most, if not all, African nations, have none. In the absence of any of these components, economic prosperity is difficult in Africa and more difficult for it, as an ideology for any meaningful national development or economic growth. This can be traced to the absence of the critical must-haves for liberal democracy to flourish – an eternally vigilant populace and an equally eternally alert political leadership. Those factors that fertilized seeds of liberalism in Western Europe were absent in Africa at the point of the independence of her nations, yet these countries were expected to use the ideology of liberalism as their compass to national development. At any event, no miracle could have put these factors on a platter for the African nations, because the instrument of colonialism which gave birth to these nations, was designed to suppress the emergence of these factors. Colonialism was fashioned to extract huge profit from trade with Africa, to create markets for its finished goods and to extract cheap labour from African countries for their labour needs at homes, not for the development of Africa. The decision to colonize Africa, after over 400 years of trade relationship, was inspired by the industrial revolution in Europe. Among other things, the industrial revolution confronted European powers with the urgent need for cheap labourers, new markets for finished products as well as uninterrupted access to raw materials for industries. Since Africa could provide all these needs, colonialism became inevitable. These were achieved at the Berlin Conference of 1884 where European powers agreed on how to partition Africa for themselves by military might. This brief historical background is important to act as a constant reminder as we progress, that colonialism was neither intended nor structured to develop Africa.

Among contemporary scholars on African development, Walter Rodney stands out for presenting a comprehensive and penetrating picture of the effect of colonialism on the development of Africa. His book, (Rodney, 1972), provides a plaintive account of what colonialism visited on the people of Africa. He touched virtually every sphere of underdevelopment in colonial Africa, covering virtually all African countries from North to South, East and West.

For our present purpose, I shall highlight three areas of interest namely: underdevelopments in infrastructure, social services (health) and education. These are areas that can still be used to measure the state of African nations more than 50 years after the end of colonialism.

In Chapter Six of his book, he recalled the grief-filled Arusha Declaration on the devastating effects of colonialism, to wit: "we have been oppressed a great deal, we have been exploited a great deal, and we have been disregarded a great deal." He proceeds from there (251 – 253) to present the gory details of colonial underdevelopment of Africa in his words: "the combination of being oppressed, being exploited and being disregarded is best illustrated by the pattern of the economic infrastructure of African countries; notably their roads and railways." Rodney explains that distribution of roads and railways, had a geographical spread according to the extent to which certain areas needed to be opened, to import/export activities. That meant that the colonial powers would cite a road or railway only in those locations where import/export thrived. In the absence of such mercantile incentives, citing of roads and railways were not considered. The implication is that roads and railways were never designed to facilitate social cohesion and integration, implying also that regions without economic import/

export values remained backward and isolated from centres of commerce within their society. Exception to these rules occurred when a few roads and railways were built for mobility of troops to make conquest easier.

Rodney further notes that means of communication were not constructed in the colonial era so that Africans could exchange visits or socialize. His words again: "There were no roads connecting different colonies and different parts of the same colony in a manner that made sense with regard to Africa's needs and development. All roads and railways led down to the sea. They were built to extract gold or manganese or coffee or cotton. They were built to make business possible for the timber companies, trading companies and agricultural concession firms and for white settlers."

Rodney continued his lament by noting that while at that time in Europe and America, capital was the prime factor of production, in Africa, labour took the lion's share in getting things done. He explained how with minimum investment of capital, the colonial powers were able to mobilize thousands upon thousands of workers. Labour, he explained, came into existence by use of colonial laws, and the threat of force and the use of force, which was why salaries were paid to police officers and officials – to use brute force to extract cheap labour.

Comparing the building of infrastructure in Europe

and America, Rodney further explained, "In Europe and America, railway building required huge inputs of capital. Great wage bills were incurred during construction and added bonus payments were made to workers to get the job done as quickly as possible. In most parts of Africa, the Europeans who wanted to see a railroad built offered lashes as the ordinary wage and more lashes for extra efforts."

This is the picture of the oppressive and extractive system of governance, employed by the colonial powers with its obvious implications for the psyche of Africans and the development of African countries. The state apparatus of colonial Africa was an instrument of inhuman coercion and brutality. It was designed for the forceful extraction of values from the African populace without regards to the rights of the victims. Africans were consequently made to see formal state structures as instruments of oppression and degradation. This image of government as represented by the white colonialists, was that of an institution that was aloof from the people, meant for a privileged few, whose coercive powers were next only to God.

This ensured a psychological disconnect between the people and the government. This impression still subsists in Africa. Citizens are still regarded with aloofness by their government, who see State power, as an instrument for the oppressive extraction of values from them.

Furthermore, that psychological disconnect between the people and the government which originated from colonialism has not waned, primarily because the African leadership that emerged after independence conducted themselves as the black version of their white masters, whom they took over from. The failure to de-link the colonial impression of statehood on the mindset of Africans many years after independence, is a major leadership failure of the political class, who have become no better than the colonial powers. The continuous recourse by African leaders to abuse of power, disregard for the rule of law and discriminatory policies, has not made them any better than the colonialists. Although we shall return to this subject as we progress, the pertinence of its mention here is to underline the fact that a disillusioned populace forced to remain disconnected to its government can hardly contribute in earnest to national development.

The use of brute force to intimidate and extract values from Africans was not the only affront that colonialism visited on Africans. The picture in the area of health and social service is even more gruesome. Rodney presents a lurid description of what happened in most African countries: "In Algeria, the figure for infant mortality was 39 per 1000 live births among white settlers, but it jumped to 170 per 1000 live births in the case of Algerians living in the township, proof that the medical maternity and sanitation services were all geared towards the wellbeing of the settlers. Similarly, in South Africa, all social statistics have to be broken down into at least two groups, white and black, if they are to be interpreted correctly. In British East Africa, there were three groups. Firstly, the Europeans who got the most, then Indians who took most of what was left, and thirdly the Africans who came last in their own country."

The skewed distribution of social service was a widespread phenomenon in virtually all colonial Africa. As Rodney further recalls, although the impression was wrongly created that the South of Nigeria received the best of attention from the colonialist, the situation in Ibadan debunked that. According to him, Ibadan, one of the heavily populated cities in Africa, had only about 50 Europeans before the Second World War. However, for this few, the British government provided a segregated hospital services of 11 beds while only 34 beds were provided for half a million blacks. The situation, in Rodney's words, "was repeated in other areas, so that altogether the 4000 Europeans in the country (Nigeria) in the 1930s had 12 modern hospitals while the African population of at least 40 million had 52 hospitals."

The implication of this paltry healthcare provision is that more Africans were vulnerable to disease and likely to die from such as a result. As Rodney further reported, in 1930, scurvy and other epidemics broke out in the Lupa gold fields of Tanganyika. Hundreds of workers died for lack of facilities and very poor wages, which was not even enough for them to feed properly. In South

Africa, the large working African population was in an even worse state. According to Rodney, as early as 1912, scarcely a single family existed in which at least one member was not dying of tuberculosis. Hospital services were so inadequate that incurable tuberculosis and other cases were simply sent home to die and spread the infection." The situation was compounded further by the fact that about 65% of African children died before reaching two years.

It is evident from these facts that the health situation of Africans under colonial rule was bad enough. So bad indeed was the situation that many of them died of curable diseases, with poor wages, hunger and poverty joining the list of woes of these colonized Africans. The practical implication of all these is that with hunger, poor healthcare and poverty ravaging the African populace, they were reduced to psychological wrecks, lacking self-esteem and confidence. In that situation, they were no better than what a late Nigerian Afro-musician called "zombies" (robots) willing to be blown in any direction by the wind. It is of course needless to add that such a populace cannot be in any position to promote, support or defend their democratic rights, for as we noted earlier, it is only an economically comfortable citizen that can afford the time and resources to protect his rights.

It is necessary to note at this point that the wealth and social conditions of a vast majority of Africans have not changed significantly since the colonial era. As we shall soon see, the difference between the colonial era and the present, is not as clear as the difference between day and night or winter and summer.

If the provision of infrastructure, social services and healthcare were wilfully used by colonial powers to hold Africans back from development, education, a well-known tool for self-actualization and national development, was even more inhumanly deployed by them.

In the first place, the colonizer never really intended providing formal Western education to the Africans. In the first forty years of colonialism, a European type school system hardly operated. It was the Christian missionaries that gave schooling to Africans in that first forty years, mainly for their own religious purposes. What colonialism did was to scuttle the thriving education industry in Africa without replacing it with a Western alternative. Evidence from history shows that before the Europeans came, an appreciable number of North Africans, Ethiopians, East and West Africans were literate. A proof of this can be seen from the fact that before colonialism, there was the All-Asher University in Egypt and the University of Timbuktu in Mali. The fact that these universities were already in Africa before the 19th century, when colonialism assassinated Africa, should rest any form of debate on availability of education in Africa before colonialism. What the colonial power did, first, indirectly, through the missionaries and later directly, was to truncate a unique African educational system that was on the ascendency and replace it with a Western education in a haphazard manner. The colonialists got interested in directly educating Africans for the sole purpose of helping to train low-ranking clerks and messengers, to help their private companies owned by their kin. Only a very small percentage of national revenue of the colonies was voted for education, clear evidence that provision of education was not a priority to the colonial powers. As Rodney (294) notes: in 1935, of the total revenue collected from taxing Africans in French West Africa, only 4.03% was utilised in education. The situation was worse in the British colony of Nigeria, where only 3.4% of revenue was voted for education. Also, as late as 1946 in Kenya, only 2.26% of total revenue was spent on education. Because of these paltry budgetary provisions for education, it was only natural that only few Africans made it into schools (mainly primary and secondary). The fact that the colonial educational system was only interested in educating Africans for the position of clerks and messengers meant that higher or tertiary education was not very necessary.

This explains why all through colonial Africa, secondary schools were very few, and most of them were owned by Christian missionaries, and universities were virtually non-existent. The few Africans who thirsted for university education had no choice but to travel to

Europe and America for that. Of course, this served the interest of the colonizer because those Africans who travelled to Europe and America to study either never returned or came back as white men in black skin, with their air of superiority.

The implication of this poorly-executed colonial education policy is that, at best, it produced a few half-educated Africans, and at worst, left a vast majority of them illiterate and ignorant. With little or no education at their disposal, these Africans could, in no way, be adjudged the best people to be positioned for apostleship of liberal democracy. They were not in a position to understand or appreciate what it stood for, and worse of all, they could not see any how the ideology could make any difference in their impoverished lives.

More disturbing is that colonial education deliberately failed to provide a curriculum that would allow Africans to acquire relevant skills. What was taught at the primary and few secondary schools available were general knowledge, European civics and history. There was no provision for any form of skill acquisition. By and large, at independence, Africa had a large number of working-age adults without skills, who were therefore more of liabilities than assets to their new nations.

This was, of course, part of the expectation of the colonizer – that even with independence, African countries with neither skilled labour nor technology, would still look up to the West for importation of finished goods, while maintaining its colonial status as a large reservoir to produce cheap labour and raw materials. If you are wondering how Africa has remained the main source of cheap labour to the West, you only need to investigate the number of Africans who continue to migrate to Europe to discover that they are in large numbers and rising by each year. As immigrants in Europe and America, these Africans gladly submit themselves for employment in menial jobs with low wages, jobs that many whites will not touch with a long spoon. That is voluntary labour by Africans, forced on them by the lingering legacy of poor socio-economic conditions bequeathed to them by colonialism.

This, to me, is akin to voluntary slavery but not as pronounced as the one achieved through the phenomenon known as US Visa Lottery for US citizenship. Those who win are given US visas and green cards with authorization to seek for employment in the US. Millions apply for this lottery every year. The few that succeed gladly travel to the US to begin the search for jobs including menial ones. This, to me, is a clear case of voluntary slavery. For an African to willingly leave his country with US visa, to go into a country unknown to him or her, in search of any available job, amounts to voluntary surrender to slavery, in my view. However, this is only possible because of the excruciating socio-economic conditions in their home countries: the home country which compels him to seek survival elsewhere at all cost, even if it means becoming a "slave."

More important is the fact that these socio-economic conditions have forced these African nations to continuously look up to the West for economic salvation. As I said earlier, this was the plot of colonialism. Without a strong productive base at home, African nations cannot produce enough to sustain themselves as independent nations. This inadequacy means depending on imports from the West for survival. This turns African nations into import-dependent nations, requiring foreign exchange which the African countries earn through the raw materials they export to the West and in some cases crude oil. This is a vicious cycle, all reminiscent of colonial lordship, where materials must be exported to the West for them to process and return to Africa as finished goods. Crude oil is a more recent example exported to the West as crude by Africans and imported back as gasoline from them. The vicious cycle goes on and on. In the process, African nations run short of foreign exchange to import and they have to borrow from IMF and Paris club etc., for a restructuring exercise that has remained elusive.

The position statement of Nigeria's former Minister of Finance, Ngozi Okonjo-Iweala, on Nigeria's economy in the 2000s, is quite like what was obtained in the colonial economy. At the very opening of her book,

(Okonjo-Iweala, 2012), she declared: "The nation was riddled with corruption, bloated with debt, battered by economic volatility. The macro economy was seriously imbalanced. A series of national institutions – the civil service, pensions, customs – were broken. Healthcare, education and other basic services were poorly delivered. Infrastructure was in disarray or disrepair. Poverty was rampart, and inequality was deep." She provided more details (920) which she said was the outcome of intense analysis of the problem prior to her assuming office in 2003. In her words: "We had inherited an unstable macro-economic environment characterized by volatile exchange rates, double digit inflation 23% on annual basis in 2003, a high fiscal deficit (3.5% GDP in 2003), low foreign exchange reserves ($US 7.5 billion in 2003), and low GDP growth (2.3% on average for the past decade including negative GDP growth per capita in those years because of increase in population)".

Apart from the technical jargons such as unstable macro-economic environment, economic volatility and so on, all she said boils down to a simple economic truth: Nigeria is not developed. The same characterization she provided for the present-day Nigerian economy will certainly apply to the immediate past colonial economy of Nigeria? The more fundamental issue is that "healthcare, education and other basic services were poorly delivered," applied to the colonial economy just the same way it applies to the Nigerian economy in the 2000s, many years after independence. That "infrastructure was in disarray or disrepair" or that "poverty was rampant, and inequality was deep" sounds more like a description of the colonial economy. Yet it was about Nigeria in the 2000s (this is the irony of Africa's quest for development). The same "macroeconomic environment" and the same "economic volatility" that colonialism created have persisted in most African countries, almost sixty years after independence. To make matters worse, African leaders, rather than seek for solutions inward, have continued to look up to the same West who brought about their nations' downfall in the first place, for solutions. This is perfectly described in the African proverb about going to the same man who shot you to extract the bullet from your body. It never works.

Part of the problem here is that imperialist institutions like the IMF and World Bank, which African countries run to for economic salvation, often end up trying to make them more amenable for Western exploitation, by giving them reform conditions that only make the matter worse. Such conditions as Okonjo-Iweala pointed out (98) will necessarily include, amongst others, implementation of economic reforms under a formal programme approved by the International Monetary Fund (IMF). In essence, the IMF will dictate the programmes which a country must implement, to qualify for assistance from the institution. Sometimes, such conditions could include, restricting public sector expenditures in such a way that jobs are cut, thereby increasing the number of helpless, unemployed poor African people. At other times, it could require the outright sale of public firms or privatization, which leads to the same outcome. A few wealthy individuals, sometimes in partnership with their Western collaborators, buy up these public assets or firms, retrench staff, and as the rank of the poor jobless increases, the few corruptly rich get richer. In the end, no progress is made on development; otherwise, there will be records showing African countries that have, through IMF assisted programmes, transited from the status of underdeveloped to developed.

The picture becomes clearer when we look at the World Bank Report on Africa GDP per capita for 2019 *(see table 5)*. The report shows that of the 54 countries surveyed, 45 or 83.3% of them belong to the category of lower middle-income countries, that is with per capita of $1,026 – 4,035 USD. Those in the upper middle income or 11.3% belong to the higher income bracket of $12,476 USD or more. What this simply means is that above 83% of African countries are still very poor, sixty-five years after many of them gained independence.

Table 5: *World Bank Report on Africa GDP per capita for 2019*

S/N	Country	Per Capita Income ($)
1	Algeria	12,019.9
2	Angola	6,965.5
3	Benin	3,432.8

S/N	Country	Per Capita Income ($)
4	Botswana	18,552.8
5	Burkina Faso	2,274.7
6	Burundi	784.9
7	Cabo Verde	7,489.2
8	Cameroon	3,803.5
9	Central African Republic	986.7
10	Chad	1,649.5
11	Comoros	3,194.9
12	Democratic Republic of the Congo	1,146.5
13	Republic of Congo	3,835.7
14	Côte d'Ivoire	5,443.2
15	Djibouti	5,779.7
16	Egypt	12,283.8
17	Equatorial Guinea	19,379.2
18	Eritrea (2011)	1,625.5
19	Eswatini	9,003.4
20	Ethiopia	2,319.7
21	Gabon	15,611.6
22	The Gambia	2,321.2
23	Ghana	5,652.2
24	Guinea	2,675.5
25	Guinea-Bissau	2,077.4
26	Kenya	4,521.5
27	Lesotho	2,824.1
28	Liberia	1,491.0
29	Libya	15,845.7
30	Madagascar	1,719.9
31	Malawi	1,106.6

S/N	Country	Per Capita Income ($)
32	Mali	2,424.3
33	Mauritania	5,427.1
34	Mauritius	23,882.4
35	Morocco	7,826.2
36	Mozambique	1,338.1
37	Namibia	10,063.6
38	Niger	1,278.7
39	Nigeria	5,362.8
40	Rwanda	2,325.4
41	São Tomé and Príncipe	4,145.2
42	Senegal	3,545.1
43	Seychelles	30,516.7
44	Sierra Leone	1,794.3
45	Somalia	N/A
46	South Africa	13,034.2
47	South Sudan (2015)	1,234.7
48	Sudan	4,122.5
49	Tanzania	2,770.7
50	Togo	1,667.3
51	Tunisia	11,231.6
52	Uganda	2,284.3
53	Zambia	3,624.0
54	Zimbabwe	2,961.4

Life expectancy in Africa, an indicator of state of health of the citizenry, is not very encouraging either. A 2015 World Health Report on life expectancy in African countries (*table* 6) shows that citizens in 37 or 78.7% of the 47 African countriess surveyed should expect to die on or before the age of 65. Only in 10 countries, 21.3%

can citizens expect to live between 65 and 74 years. This is a very sharp contrast from what we saw of European countries in the previous chapter, where the lowest life expectancy is 71 years in East Europe.

Table 6: *Life Expectancy Africa (Africa Kitoko, 2020)*

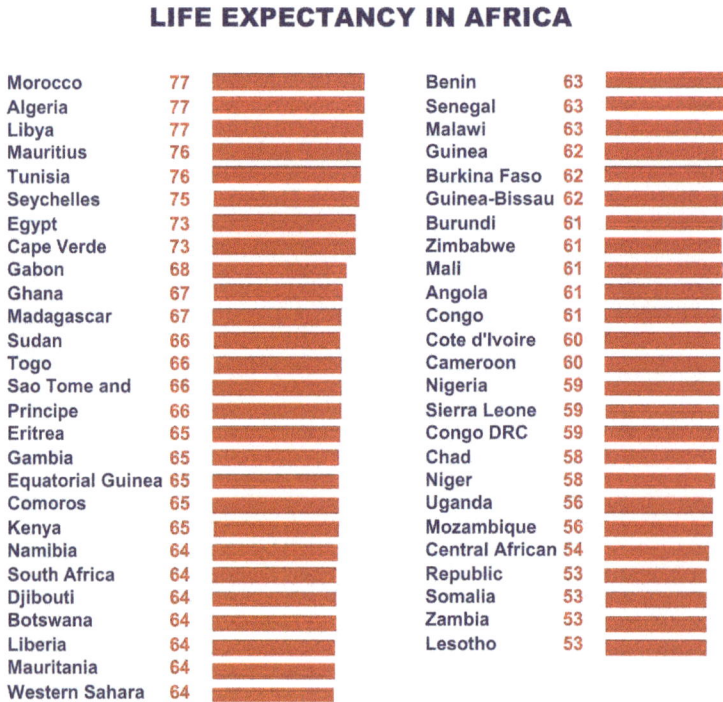

LIFE EXPECTANCY IN AFRICA

Country	Value		Country	Value	
Morocco	77		Benin	63	
Algeria	77		Senegal	63	
Libya	77		Malawi	63	
Mauritius	76		Guinea	62	
Tunisia	76		Burkina Faso	62	
Seychelles	75		Guinea-Bissau	62	
Egypt	73		Burundi	61	
Cape Verde	73		Zimbabwe	61	
Gabon	68		Mali	61	
Ghana	67		Angola	61	
Madagascar	67		Congo	61	
Sudan	66		Cote d'Ivoire	60	
Togo	66		Cameroon	60	
Sao Tome and	66		Nigeria	59	
Principe	66		Sierra Leone	59	
Eritrea	65		Congo DRC	59	
Gambia	65		Chad	58	
Equatorial Guinea	65		Niger	58	
Comoros	65		Uganda	56	
Kenya	65		Mozambique	56	
Namibia	64		Central African	54	
South Africa	64		Republic	53	
Djibouti	64		Somalia	53	
Botswana	64		Zambia	53	
Liberia	64		Lesotho	53	
Mauritania	64				
Western Sahara	64				

In Western Europe, as we saw, a citizen should not expect to die before the age of 80. Many Africans are still liable to die young, just like in the colonial era, when Africans were yet to have healthcare delivery services that their citizens could be proud of. It is quite conclusive that Africa has remained largely underdeveloped since independence and the reasons are rather obvious. Most African countries have tried to apply liberalism as a means of governance and development. We have seen that the factors that fertilize liberal ideology to fruition are starkly absent in Africa.

Such factors as we outlined earlier are knowledgeable populace, independent and critical media, strong institutions that can support the implementation of free and fair elections, and they are absent in Africa. If there were strong institutions to support free and fair elections, bloodletting and ballot snatching as witnessed in the 2016 and 2017 re-run elections in Rivers State of Nigeria, would not occur. In like manner, the 2016 political debacle in Gambia, where an incumbent President, after his defeat in an election, refused to vacate his seat, requiring the threat of a regional West African force to shove him out, would not have occurred. Nor would a man have remained in office for over 30 years as the President of Zimbabwe.

Some optimists may want to argue that the threat of West African military intervention in Gambia, which forced out the defeated President, is an indication that the required institution would eventually grow in Africa to support free and fair elections. My answer is that what happened in the Gambia was only possible because of the size of that country. It is doubtful that it can happen with bigger West African countries such as Nigeria or Ghana.

African countries also lack independent and critical media, a vital institution for the defence of liberal democracy. Most media firms in Africa are owned by the government, and even the ones owned by private individuals depend largely on government patronage for survival. Again, in Africa, most private media owners are politicians who have vested interest in politics. A combination of these factors makes it difficult for the media to be independent and patriotic in Africa. Besides, the medium of communication is English or French, two languages that a majority of ignorant Africans do not understand deep enough to enable them profit constructively from mass media information.

In the absence of these factors that help to lubricate the wheels of liberal democracy by checking the excesses of rulers, political leaders gradually slip into the embrace of the attraction of dictatorship. Power, being an opium of sorts, begins to intoxicate them slowly, and steadily they become more of "democratic monarchs" than elected leaders. These problems will persist and Africa's underdeveloped status will linger for as long as Africans continue to look up to a wholesale application of liberalism as a solution to their development needs. What needs to be done, and perhaps urgently too, is to look inwards and find a sensitive democratic system or an Africanized liberal ideology that can stimulate the interest of the populace in governance and stimulate growth as well. This is the task that Econocracy is set to accomplish in the next chapter.

Chapter 6

THE TASK BEFORE ECONOCRACY

In the course of this work, we have identified some components that we can rightly describe as the basic factors that can facilitate natural development. Democracy is key in this respect because the instance of North and South Korea, and East and West Europe, which were highlighted in preceding chapters, clearly demonstrate the fact that an open and free market helps nations develop faster and better in contrast to a closed centralized market. We also saw that democracy, as espoused in liberal democratic ideas has worked in Western countries, where it evolved from in the first place, but has not quite worked in Africa, where it was imposed. Again we saw that for Africa to move forward to development, she must look inwards and modify the liberal democratic ideology, or put differently, Africanize liberalism. Our investigation was conclusive also that the factors that help to fertilize liberalism to the fruition of national development include a knowledgeable electorate, independent and critical media, free and fair elections, and strong democratic institutions.

The foregoing leads me to the next stage, which is the task before Econocracy, something that it must resolve to define: a pathway to development in Africa. We already know that Econocracy stands for economic democracy, an ideology that seeks to place man's economic rights before his civil or political rights. Furthermore, it is an ideology, that postulates the superiority of the economic needs of man, as the forerunner of his political rights. Broken down, it means that it is only when man's economic needs are secured, that his political rights can be defended. The position is that political rights without economic security, are at best a whitewash or a paper tiger, which in the words of William Shakespeare is "full of sound and fury, signifying nothing."

This being so, I proceed to set the task before Econocracy, first in a broad sense, then to the specifics. The broad sense is the urgent need for backward integration, that is, to find a way for the political environment to connect with the people and stimulate their interest in the polity or the political process. As we also saw in previous chapters, a major bane of the political process in African nations is the disconnect between the people and the political elite.

This broad approach evolves, looking at Econocracy as the ideology for stimulating a strong state organ, that will focus on economic development in African nations. This can be achieved by focusing on competitive production, intra-African trade and creating the enabling environment, that will protect intra-African trade and allow it to grow before opening to outsiders.

It sounds obvious that the only way an economy can grow and sustain growth is by maintaining appreciable productive capacity. Two areas that colonialism fatally damaged the African economy are firstly, through its degrading of the African culture and supplanting it with European values. This is felt most in the areas of food, culture and fashion. Most Africans have been sold deeply to European food culture that Africa has become a dumping ground for every type of European food, including sausage and all manner of pasteurized food items. In the African Fashion industry, everything Western is preferred to everything African by many Africans, from T-shirts to short and long trousers, to women's clothes, suits including artificial hairs etc. The second area is the intra-Africa trade, which Rodney rightly noted as having been booming before the Berlin Conference. Colonialism dealt a deadly blow to this trade, which could have served and can still serve as catalyst for Africa's development. We shall return to this trade issue shortly, but first, let us look at the food and fashion industry challenge.

The underpinning philosophy of econocracy is to reverse those losses and bounce them back as springboards for African development, by cooperating with each other. African countries can promote intra-Africa food delicacies and encourage each other to export them to other countries. The same can happen in the fashion/textile industry. African nations can encourage local fabric manufacturers to come out with excellent designs. An African touch that would appeal to African countries, with special skills in this area, encouraged to specialize in producing these fine African fabrics, that can compete with international standards. The same would go for footwear and accessories.

To achieve this, every country would be encouraged to establish a National Economic Development Bank (NEDB), that will provide soft loan for entrepreneurs in the food and fashion industry. With an African Development Bank (ADB) already in place, the NEDB will work with it to explore ways of attracting capital investment, mainly from Africans, to Africa. These banks (NEDB and ADB) will continually, through research, seminars, and workshops, seek to explore and expose investment opportunities in Africa, to African capitalists. They should also provide expert advice on how to nurture the investment from seed to fruition. The objective here, as noted earlier, is to encourage inflows of capital investment to Africa. The intra-African trade is an important component of the envisaged development stimuli package. Intra-Africa trade was flourishing before the advent of colonialism; Rodney (49) notes that Africa had many trade owners that covered huge distances like routes across the Sahara, or the routes connected with Katanga Copper, all amounting to trade between neighbouring or not-too-distant societies. He explains that such trades were a funding for production, noting that "various communities were producing surplus of given commodities which could be exchanged for items which they lacked. In that way, the salt industry of one locality would be stimulated while the iron industry would be encouraged in another. In coastal lake or riverine areas, dried fish could become profitable, while yams and millet would be grown in abundance elsewhere to provide a basis for exchange."

Econocracy envisages the revival of this intra-Africa trade by encouraging specialization in areas of comparative advantage and by adopting a zero tariff for international trade among African nations. We shall revisit this later to appreciate the tremendous effect it will have on the development of African nations. In the meantime, let us examine the specifics through which the Econocracy ideology can complement its broad objectives in stimulating economic growth in Africa.

This can be specifically addressed by:

1.   Reigniting the communal African spirit as a platform for political recruitment and the enactment of a strong state institution for development
2.   Implementing compulsory mass education programme for skill acquisition
3.   Limiting Western style electoral process for elections to the legislative arm
4.   Creating statutory rights groups to reinforce democratic institutions.

I now proceed to add details to each specific.

Reigniting African Communal spirit as platform for political Recruitment

Communalism is a basic ingredient in all African societies, and it is somewhat unique to them. The ideology of extended family and kinship dominate the communal spirit of Africa. In pre-colonial era, it was the basis for deployment and distribution of means of production; land, for instance, was a collective property of different kin in the traditional Africa society who also helped in their cultivation of agriculture. The Spirit of good neighbourliness characterized the extended family system in African people. They always saw those belonging to the same kind, leverage as their kits and kin or brothers, and would always be willing to be of any assistance. There was also a competitive spirit among the kindred, which fostered development within the African environment. Communal labour was often employed to clear land or build houses, to enhance productivity. Villages often resorted to communal farming, hunting, or fishing to feed themselves. Trade between communities also boomed.

Walter Rodney (43) noted that all history is transition from one stage to the other, that even European history also transited from a form of communalism to feudalism etc. The African situation is not different; Rodney also noted that these principles of family kinship and deferment to age, "were slowly breaking down throughout the continent, preceding the arrival of the Europeans in their sailing ships." He attributed their transitioning process to changes in technology and division of labour. But for the intervention of colonialism, Africa could probably have continued her own evolutionary ladder, to an eventual developed status. I am not in any way advocating a return to this pre-colonial era, because that will be both unrealistic and illogical; however, there is yet something that can be borrowed from it. The main fabric of the African communal system is the spirit behind it: a spirit of trust, reliance on one another and confidence in the honesty of the community. This can become a rallying point for social mobilization in Africa. My proposal is that this communal spirit should be revived as the hub of economic activities at all levels of society: community, local, state and national. My submission is that the communal system is the best social force to use in actualizing individual economic rights. This is in line with Adam Smith's argument that an economic system should be based on individual self-interest. Consequently, the individual should be allowed to determine his economic interest at the community, local, state and national levels. This should be achieved through an economic council at each level.

I propose that there be a Community Economic Council (CEC) at the community level. The membership shall be drawn from adults (from ages 18 and above), each kindred making up the community. Depending on the number of kindreds that make up a community and their size (population), each kindred shall nominate not less than two and not more than five persons as members of the CEC. No CEC shall have membership strength of more than fifty. Each CEC, liaising with the different kindreds through their members, shall draw up the economic needs of the community, covering such areas as infrastructural needs of roads, electricity, portable water, communications, etc. to other social services such as health delivery. The needs should include employment and skill acquisition needs. All the needs shall be properly articulated and collated for the next stage, which is the Local Area Economic Council (LAEC).

Local area represents the Local Authority area covering a set of autonomous communities like Local Government area in Nigeria. Each CEC shall elect two members to the LAEC who shall become members of the council. The Community Economic Council member of the LAEC shall then table the articulated economic needs of their respective CECs where they shall be aggregated into the economic needs of the local authority area. They should reflect the needs of every community within the area. At the LEAC level, additions can be made to reflect the common needs of the area that could have been omitted at the CEC level, such as inter-communal roads etc. A neat document reflecting the needs of the LAEC will thereafter be prepared for forwarding to the State (Regional) Economic Council (SEC). Each LAEC shall elect one person to the SEC. This means that SEC membership shall be determined by the number of LAECs in the State or Region. The function of the SEC shall be similar to that of the LAEC, that is, to aggregate the economic needs of the LAEC and add more needs if necessary, to accommodate inter-LAEC needs. Finally, the SECs will forward the articulated economic needs of the States or Regions to a National Economic Council (NEC). The NEC can also add to these needs to accommodate inter-state needs or national economic needs.

All the economic council members shall have a ten-year tenure, that is, the CEC, the LAEC, the SEC, the

NEC. Each of them shall have a chairman to be elected by the members. None of the chairmen shall be eligible for election as a representative of his council at the next council level. That is to say, the chairman of a CEC shall not be the same person representing that council in the LAEC.

The above is one aspect of the economic councils. The other is that they shall also serve as a political recruitment platform. This means that those who want to run for elective position into any executive arm of the government, shall belong to the membership of these councils at any level. For instance, if someone wants to run for local government council chairman or mayor, as the case maybe, or governor of a state, then he must first be a member of the CEC, the LAEC or SEC. The practical implication is that any person interested in any executive elective office, must first subject himself to community scrutiny, where members of his kindred who know him best should first nominate him as a member of his CEC. The purpose of this is to ensure that those who seek to govern at any executive level can pass the test of character of his own kinsmen; after all, charity should begin at home. A person who cannot be considered by his own kinsmen as one of the five to represent his kindred at the CEC is very unlikely to be a good character.

The next stage is the role the economic councils shall play in the electoral process, particularly for the election of the executive arm and the execution of economic programme of the councils. Those seeking to govern at state level, for instance, shall after indicating interest, subject themselves to primary elections by the CEC and the LAEC. Any person who wins majority of votes cast at the primaries at Community Economic Council (CEC) and Local Area Economic Council (LAEC) becomes the candidate for governorship elections. He shall then present himself to all the voters within the state for a yes or no vote to ratify him a Governor. This should be supervised by an electoral body of that state.

If he/she loses by Yes or No vote, the entire process will be repeated until a governor emerges. One thing that must have become clear at this stage is that political parties are not involved in this electoral process. At the legislative level, political parties will be involved. The idea here is to ensure that those who emerge as the executive owe all their allegiance to the people through the Economic Councils and not to any political party. The same process shall apply for the election of council chairmen.

Also, in the executive functions proper, the governor will draw at least 70% of cabinet from the economic councils, either from the CEC, the LAEC or the SEC. This is to ensure that the focus of the executive arm of government remains on the implementation of the economic agenda drawn up by the Economic Councils. As a matter of fact, the campaign thrust of a candidate for executive position, both at the primaries and general election, shall be on how he plans to implement the economic agenda of the council within his tenure. Each elected executive shall serve a seven year tenure and a maximum of two tenures. The second important element is that all through a governor's tenure, for instance, his annual budgets must reflect the stated needs of the people, spread in an even and fair manner, as resources can carry. If the people want roads, electricity, and employment the government must make budgetary provision to incorporate these, it is also taken as a given that a component of economic ideology that will be compulsory is mass education for skill acquisition. There will be more on the skill acquisition programme as we progress.

Let me attempt to break down all we have outlined so far before moving to the National Economic Council Stage. Let us assume that in a state, all the aggregate economic needs of all the LAECs come to employment for 2000 people, construction of a 100-kilometre road network and the provision of electricity for 100 communities. The government can spell out how it plans to achieve a given percentage of all or some of these, say 10-20% within its tenure. The important thing here is that the government shall not be at liberty to draw up any programme outside the stated needs of the people. The second thing is that these are the programme of the Economic Councils, of which the governor and his cabinet are members. They will either stick to the implementation of these programmes or risk a vote of no confidence which can remove them from office. The most important thing is that when these programmes are implemented incrementally as resources allow, the people shall be carried along, knowing that it is their own programmes which go directly to the root of their economic problems. This way, the political apathy among the populace and the disconnect between the political elite and the masses will begin to abate.

At the national level, the person who shall be the chairman of the NEC shall also double as the ceremonial president of the country. His election shall be similar to the election of the governor of a state in the sense that he shall hold primaries in all the SECs in the country. The winner shall then present himself or herself to the entire electorate for a yes or no vote to ratify his election as the chairman of NEC and ceremonial president of the country. Should he lose by a NO vote, the process will be repeated for a fresh candidate until a YES vote is secured. The cabinet member of the National government shall be constituted by NECs. Each state shall nominate a ministerial candidate for the national cabinet or in some cases two, depending on the size of the State. However, the ministerial nominees must not necessarily be members of the state NEC, but once nominated and made a minister, he or she becomes an automatic member of the State NEC. In the case of the National Cabinet, the Prime Minister (we shall see how he is elected shortly), shall be a member of the cabinet as the head of government. Several implications are apparent going by this process. The chairman of the National Economic Council and Ceremonial President of the country shall not be sponsored by a political party. He will only require a yes vote from the populace to be ratified chairman of NEC and President of the country. Critics may be guided to argue that this process is not truly democratic as the chairman/president is elected by the ECs and presented to the electorate as fait accompli. That argument can only come from those living in the illusion that Western style democracy is sacrosanct. However, a yes or no vote by the electorate still ensures that the chairman/president is elected by universal adult suffrage.

Two concerns inform this approach, which is a response to the needs of the unique African environment. The fact is that the doctrine of separation of powers is deemed important by the party system. What checks and balances can really take place in a situation where the executive and legislative are members of the same party? In Africa, it has not worked because the politician will always orchestrate the idea of supremacy of the party to garage the oversight function of the legislature over the executive. Even in the Western Countries, the party system remains a major roadblock to the effective exercise of the checks and balances envisaged by the separation of powers. In Africa in particular, party interest can sometimes be placed above public interest, especially if one party controls both the executive and the legislature. Africans need an executive arm that is not incumbered by party loyalty, but which can at the same time be put in check by a legislature that is sponsored by political parties.

The second concern is that if Africa must focus on development, then those who articulate the economic needs of the people should really be allowed to execute them without loyalty to a political party, which could derail their focus. The idea is to ensure that they remain firmly focused and truly close to the people who they are accountable to, and not a political party. The process of their election is also designed to ward off the unnecessarily high expenditure that a political party-sponsored electoral process begets. Again, being members of these ECs that elects them at the primaries, will keep them focused on bringing development to their communities, who will also hold them accountable for failure. This will make them more likely to resist monetary inducements than those involved in political party primaries.

I have made the argument in my book, (Emelumba, Reinventing Nigeria: The Plebiscitarian Option, 2016), that Africa must adopt democracy to suit their environment. As we also saw earlier in this book, democracy is not an all-purpose shoe size that fits every foot. The idea of using CEs as electoral college for the election of the executive arm of government should be the African version of democracy. Has any African even fathomed why a Presidential candidate can win most votes cast in the US Presidential election and still end up not being elected the US President, as it happened between Hilary Clinton and Donald Trump? Hilary Clinton had a total of two million votes above Donald Trump's votes, but she ended up not winning the presidency because Trump had 304 Electoral College votes while she had 227. In the US, what elects a president is the number of Electoral College votes, not popular votes.

That is America's own version of democracy, fashioned to suit their peculiar needs. And so far, it has been working for them.

In passing, I mentioned earlier on that judges are not elected in most liberal democratic countries. The judiciary is a very important arm, and its members are appointed. No one has ever seen this as falling short of democratic standards; instead, it is justified by the argument that it is a specialized assignment that requires thorough bred professionals to man. The same argument should go for the Executive arm of government. It is a special assignment for the development of Africa, and it requires committed people who should not be distracted by partisan consideration.

Let me also make it clear that this arrangement does not contradict the Plebiscitarian Option in my first book. The approach, although focusing on economic development, still carries the people along through inbuilt recourses to the Plebiscite, which is what my first book is about. *Diagram 3* below illustrates the Economic Council (EC) chain from the kindred layer to the Community, State and National.

Diagram 3: *Economic Council Chain*

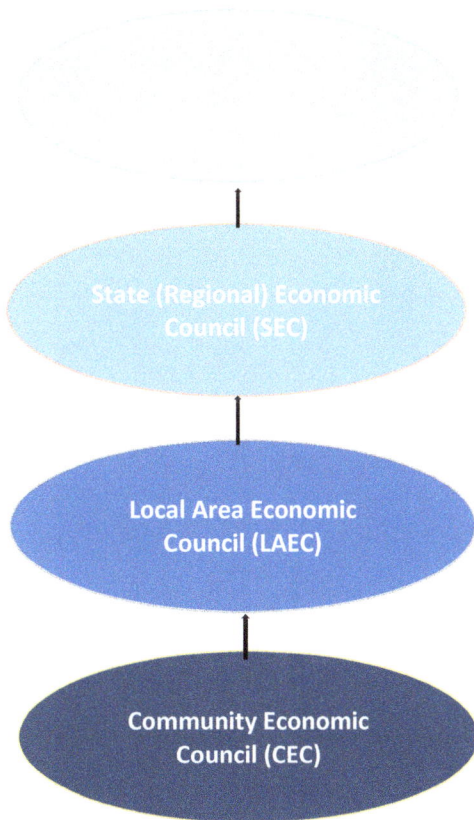

Another issue that may agitate the mind of critics is the question of the ten-year tenure for the CEs and what guarantees against the members getting corrupt or abusing their powers in the process, or even, for that matter, since the members are not economic experts, how best they can really identify and execute the economic interest of the people.

Starting from the last worry, my response is that executive arms of governments anywhere in the world are not exactly elected because of their expertise in either economic matters or development needs of the people. I agree that leaders should be knowledgeable – and the members of CEs should be – but they do not need to be experts to make good leaders. However, because their charge is specific to economic or national development, the State and National CEs shall have Secretariats and experts and professionals, that will advise the council and regulate organized seminars and workshops to update them with developmental issues. The State secretariat should serve all the CEs in the state and there should be cooperation and co-ordination between the state CE Secretariat manned by the National CE Secretariat.

On the guarantee against corruption and abuse of office, the members of CEs shall be made to understand and accept from day one that there is a call to service, not for personal enrichment or aggrandizement or for the pursuit of imperial ego. To this end, they shall, as part of their oath of office, be subjected to oaths of honesty, transparency, and accountability. They shall, as a result, be required to publicly declare their assets upon becoming members of the ECs and to repeat the exercise every year until the end of their tenure. They shall also undertake to voluntarily prohibit themselves or family members from seeking any form of medical treatment abroad while in office. Two reasons make this requirement mandatory. The first is that as public officers, medical treatment abroad would automatically mean that the government will foot the bill, whereas the same government will not do so for an ordinary citizen, implying that the health of an elected government official is more important than that of an average citizen.

The ideology of Econocracy is designed to abolish this imperialist mentality. The second reason is that by not seeking medical treatment abroad, the government shall be forced to develop the health delivery service at home to the benefit of the greater number of people. Those who may want to point out that this could amount to an abridgment of a citizen's democratic right should be reminded that there are democracies, including that of the West, that have had good reason to abridge citizens democratic rights. An opinion on this issue, retrieved from the website for liberal democracy, drives this point home: "In practice, democracies do have limits on certain freedoms. There are various legal limitations such as copyright laws and laws against defamation. There may be limits on anti-democratic speech or attempts to undermine human rights, and on the promotion of justification of terrorism. In the United States, more than in Europe, during the cold war, such restrictions applied to organizations perceived as promoting actual terrorism or the incitements of group hatred. Examples include anti-terrorism legislation, the shutting down of Hezbollah Satellite broadcast and some laws against hate speech."

Any member of the EC accused of stealing from the public treasury shall be deemed to have been accused of armed robbery and so, shall stand trial in accordance with the relevant laws of his country regarding armed robbery. If convicted, such a person shall be sent to serve the same sentence applicable to armed robbers. The rationale for this is that the same argument for armed robbery can be applied to a public officer who steals from public funds. An armed robber is a person who robs another with the force of arms. When we talk of force and arms, no person in any country has more force or arms than the State. What differentiates a state apparatus from any other organization is its entitlement to the legitimate use of force or coercion for the enforcement of its action or policies. Acemoglu and Robinson, quoting Max Weber (80), find the State as having "the monopoly of legitimate violence in society." It follows that someone charged with the running of an institution, that can legitimately use coercion, force, or violence to achieve its designs, who then turns around to use the platform of that same institution to rob the public, is guilty of armed robbery if convicted. He or she should therefore face the same sentence that awaits another citizen, who uses force or arms to rob his fellow countryperson. This provision will emphatically serve as clear notice of deterrence to those who may want to use their position in the EC to steal public funds. In addition, it will ensure that only those truly committed to service will serve in the ECs.

On the issue of the ten-year tenure, some may argue that it is too long a period to stay in office without revalidating a mandate. My response is that even the Western democratic system that is forced down our throats is not fixated on tenures. Tenures vary from country to country. In France, the President stays for seven years before going back to the electorate. Germany is the same. United Kingdom and Canada do not really have fixed tenures. The Executive and Legislature can rule forever for as long as they have the confidence of the people. Yes, they periodically revalidate their mandates, but there is no fixed tenure.

Talking about fixed tenure and revalidation of mandates, what happens to the British, Spanish, or Belgian

Monarchies in Europe? They are never elected but stay in office for life. Notwithstanding this obvious undemocratic element, the United Kingdom is in fact classified as one of the advanced democracies in the West, and other countries respect them as such.

My position is that the tenure of a government should reflect the needs, aspirations, and culture of the people. There should be no fixation about it. African countries need a secure tenure to implement long term economic policies that can impact the lives of her people. For African countries, a situation where many elections are held every four years is disruptive and avoidable. African countries do not have the necessary institutional resilience and framework to absorb these election-induced challenges, and still make progress in governance and sustainable development. This explains the rationale for the ten-year tenure, which at any event is also democratic.

This brings us to the next specific.

Limiting Western Type of Election to The Legislature

A major component of liberal democracy, as noted earlier, is periodic elections. In most western democracies, elections are held every four years, or in some cases like France and Germany, every seven years. But that is only to form the executive arm of government. Elections into the legislative arm also vary from country to country, depending on the tenure of the legislative. In the US, house of representative members are elected every two years while that of senators is every four years. In France and Germany, it is every four years for legislative, while in the United Kingdom and Canada, it is every five years at the maximum, because by a vote of no confidence, the parliament can be dissolved ahead of the expiration of its tenure and fresh elections held. The point here is that the tenure of the legislative arms of government in western democracies, and the time for their elections vary from country to country. This implies that what Econocracy envisages for legislative tenure of five years is in tandem with the practice in the West. The difference, however, is that it is only legislative election that will hold every five years, along party lines by universal adult suffrage.

Political parties are the organizations that will sponsor candidates for election into the legislative arm. As we have already seen, the Executive arm will not be sponsored by political parties but by the structures of Econocracy, subject to a ratification through a referendum for yes or no vote for the candidate that emerges from these structures. As a law-making organ, the legislatures' main concern here shall be to enact the relevant laws that will promote economic development, or put differently, to provide the legislative framework for the implementation of the ideology of Econocracy. Consequently, political parties that sponsor them should be able to convince the voters that they identify with this ideology and have the necessary vision to employ legislative instruments for its implementation. This is to ensure that the legislature is made to buy into the ideology of Econocracy.

At the end of the election, the party that secures the highest number of seats in the National parliament shall produce a Prime Minister for the country. The Prime Minister shall also be a member of the cabinet as the coordinating minister, to serve as the direct link between the Executive and the Legislature, and to brief the legislature regularly on government business, including fiscal policies and budgets. To reduce the influence of money in parliamentary elections, the public should bear the finances of both the political parties and the electoral process. This system, which I call "An Investment Theory approach", is well laid out in my book, (Emelumba, *Election Finance and Corruption in Nigeria: An Investment Theory Approach*, 2017). A major component of this approach is the establishment of civil society electoral process monitors, by laws, to facilitate the enforcement of electoral laws limiting the finance of political parties and election to the public by ensuring that offenders are prosecuted. I identified these organizations as Election Action Committees (EAC), in my book in a reference modelled after the Political Action Committees (PAC) in the US. This approach will be quite helpful in sanitizing the electoral process and reducing public sector corruption. More importantly, it will help to ensure that the legislative arm of government is attuned to the econocratic ideology of governance.

Compulsory Mass Education Programme for Skill Acquisition

It will be needless to emphasize that education – more importantly, skill oriented education – is the key to rapid national development. We already saw that an ignorant populace is a liability to the development of a country. What we are to see in the next chapter, is that this type of education, helped the East Asian countries to fast forward National development. Literacy level may be appreciating in African countries, but the truth is that most of the education in African countries, provide only basic general Western type of education without the relevant technological skills that can stimulate growth in the Africa economic environment. There is need for a general overhaul of the Africa education system to fill this yearning gap.

One way of doing this is by establishing a skills acquisition centre in every state or region in an African country. In each centre, emphasis should be on those skill areas in which the populace has comparative advantage. For instance, in the South Eastern part of Nigeria, Abia State is noted for its footwear and fashion industry. A skills acquisition centre in the footwear and fashion industry can be set up in this area. The Secretariat of the State EC shall identify areas of comparative skill advantage within the state and advise accordingly on the type of Skill Acquisition Centre (SAC) to be set up there. These centres shall have intermediate and advanced levels. Graduates from tertiary and secondary schools, whose training does not equip them enough for immediate self-employment, shall be trained in the SAC to ensure that they have a certificate of proficiency in on skill set, such as soap making, tailoring, metal fabrication, animal husbandry, food processing, etc. Upon graduation, the National Development Bank will mandatorily offer them soft loans to kick-start their own business, which the bank will regularly supervise to ensure good management. Others who can fit into regular employment of bigger companies requiring services in their area of skill specialization shall be free to secure employment with such firms.

If this programme is assiduously implemented, the difference in the productive capacity of the African country concerned will be manifest within the first ten years; more importantly, the substance of this programme in subsequent years will most likely break the jinx of many years of near-zero development in Africa. At this juncture, it is necessary that we see from the next chapter that a combination of these factors, including nonadherence to World Bank and IMF conditionalities for assistance in development, helped East Asian countries developed faster than other developing countries.

Chapter 7

LESSONS FROM EAST ASIA & LATIN AMERICA

A study of economic growth in East Asia and Latin America reveals a sharp contrast between remarkable success on one hand and no less remarkable failure on the other. East Asian countries, particularly the four Tigers, adopted a rather homegrown development model driven by economic nationalism, and developed at a rate that baffled observers and analysts. On the other hand, most of Latin America embraced Western liberal ideology as a development model and ended up with countries in stagnation and poverty. The countries in the region that toed the line of socialist development models did not fare any better either. They too ended up with stunted economic growth and poverty.

As we shall see, the major difference is that most Asian countries turned their backs on the development conditionality of international organizations such as IMF and World Bank. Instead, they invented a unique model of development in response to their peculiar needs and environment. This was the magic and it made quite a tremendous difference in their development strides and took the lead in industrialization within the region. The colony developed strong textile and manufacturing industries in the early 1960s, through which it made a mark as a world financial centre in the 1970s. Closely following in the industrialization drive were Taiwan, South Korea and Singapore, who in the 1990s joined Japan as developed economies in South East Asia.

Although China may have been a latecomer in the development stride of South East Asian economies, she is presently receiving global attention as the emerging dominant economy of the region. By 2016, many analysts considered Japan, South Korea, Taiwan and Hong Kong as the four East Asian countries that have most developed markets by most economic indices, while Singapore was the sole developed market in South East Asia. However, since 2010, when China became the world's second largest economy, attention on growth in East Asia has shifted to her. In spite of this, the fact remains that the Asian Tigers are not relenting in their development strides. A 2012 report by *The Economist* predicted that South Korea will overtake Japan in terms of GDP per person at Power Purchasing Parity (PPP) by 2017. Incidentally, this feat had already been accomplished by Taiwan in 2010 and Hong Kong in 1997.

The fact of the matter is that the four Asian Tigers had very high growth rates and speedy industrialization. They grew rich very quickly and today, they are counted among the developed economies of the world. It can indeed be said that since 1960, the Asian continent, which incidentally is the largest and most populous of the continents, has grown at a far greater speed than any other continent in the world. For over a 30-year period since 1960, the Asian Tigers have had an amazing annual growth per capita in excess of 6%, while China and Japan have maintained growth rates of 3-5%.

It is crystal clear that the East Asian countries, particularly the Asian Tigers, developed at a rather fascinating rate. Our interest, in this study, is to determine why this was so, particularly given the fact that their approach to development differed significantly from the Western models of development, IMF and World Bank development prescriptions for developing countries.

What Happened? And How Did it Happen?

These appear to be the main thrust of our concern here. However, with respect to the first question, we already have the answer, which is that the Asian Tigers developed faster than any continent has ever done. Our concern then shall be to see how this happened.

In his paper, (Ohno, 2002), Kenichi Ohno observed that the unique features of East Asia growth is that it has been attained through the very existence of East Asia as a powerful arena of economic interaction among its members, and not merely by market friendly policies or good governance of individual countries alone.

What is more striking is that the development model of these East Asian countries did not conform to the conditionality of IMF or World Bank, yet nonconformity helped them to achieve desired results. According to Ohno, "East Asia, as a region, has offered a political, economic and social model and an enabling environment for the catching up of latecomer countries. Every country (in East Asia) was under strong market pressure from above and below to constantly improve capabilities and climb the ladders of development. What drove them were national desire for material well-being and the demonstration of excellence from neighbouring countries, not conditionality or policy matrices introduced by the international organizations. Other developing regions have formed such an organic dynamic interdependence as East Asia."

Two essentials stand out in this respect, namely regional integration and cooperation and the adoption of a unique development model driven by national needs and not conditionality of IMF and World Bank. The East Asian countries saw themselves as belonging to a chain in the production network that encouraged competition and cooperation amongst themselves along the lines of comparative advantage. This meant that to stimulate development, they had to embrace international integration through trade and investment. In essence, the East Asian countries developed the region into an economic block where countries were encouraged to freely trade and invent within the region, thereby bringing out the best competitive capability in each country. The consequence of this competitive pressure was that these countries were able to upgrade their industrial capability from low-tech to high-tech. This is but a natural fallout of any healthy competition. To have competitive edge, countries will be forced to concentrate on those production lines, where they have comparative advantage, in the confidence that a regional market can provide a ready market for their products. Naturally, such competition will lead to improved skills which will in turn lead to higher and faster production. In such a situation, it is the competitive pressure, made robust by a ready regional market, that drives production and growth, and not conditionality from international agencies. This was partly responsible for the incredible growth rate of the East Asian Tigers.

The role of government was yet another crucial factor in the progress made by the Asian Tigers. As argued by Ohno, simply deregulating and opening up the private sector will not generate sufficient impetus for growth in a country saddled with underdeveloped markets, lack of human resources, low or zero technology and low productivity. He explained that in order to kick-start an economy trapped in the vicious circle of low income, low saving and low technology, the role of government is crucial as an external agent imparting order and direction to the national economy. Something remarkable about the role the government of the Asian Tigers played in developing their countries was the discipline they exhibited, which was in response to the development stages of their country, and the needs of their region. Each government was conscious of the fact that failure to act appropriately would mean that the country will be left behind in the competitive regional arena and may remain stagnant and unable to join the regional productive network. The role of government was therefore crucial and sensitive. It can be argued, as Ohno did, that because of the special circumstance of the Asian Tiger countries, and because each country's government must be proactive and Spartan in its actions, good governance must also be redefined in the East Asian context.

Consequently, "the usual components of good governance, such as macroeconomic stability, structured reform, administrative efficiency and transparency, social participation and the like, do not necessarily coincide with the conditions needed for growth driven by trade and investment. Among them, macroeconomic stability is certainly a must. But for the other components, East Asia has achieved high growth without them. It is possible that different and more sharply defined components of good governance are required to initiate growth under international integration."

The point here is that East Asian countries did not allow themselves to be bugged down by the fine details of definition of good governance, structural reform, administrative efficiency, and transparency, etc., which are usually contained in IMF and World Bank conditionalities for development. East Asia achieved growth without them, and what that tells us is that these conditionalities are the products of a development model fixation anchored on the liberal ideology of the West. Applying them unadulterated, as many developing countries are wont to do, has not been able to take any underdeveloped country to any appreciable level of development, as we shall also see in the case of Latin American countries. The reasons are not far-fetched, and we have mentioned them earlier: liberal ideology is a Western European phenomenon, an epoch in its history, not any universal strategy for economic development. It serves the purpose of the West because of the historical realities that brought it forth. It may not serve any other continent as well as it served them.

This historical reality evidently informed the departure of the East Asian countries with respect to their approach to national development. Not surprisingly, the basic challenge of the East Asian governments was the establishment of stable political regimes and social cohesion, which are the conditions of economic development. For this purpose, most countries in East Asia chose authoritarian developmentalism for authoritarianism with capability.

Ohno explains that this type of regime is quite different from a dictatorship, and went ahead to outline the features of the regime to include:

i.   Economic nationalism in pursuit of material prosperity

ii.   Obsession with external competitiveness under industrialization and export orientation.

iii.   Top-down decision making under a powerful and economically literate leader and supporting elite group.

He went ahead to note that such regimes are not "democratic" by Western standards, but that its adoption was motivated by the need to initiate growth in the regional environment. It is necessary, at this juncture, to draw attention to the fact that the above outline of an authoritarian developmentalist government fits into my Econocracy ideology in more ways than one. Economic nationalism in pursuit of material prosperity is at the centre of the establishment of the ECs under Econocracy. The focus of the ECs is to pursue material prosperity of the citizenry. As we saw earlier, material prosperity is, by the outline of Econocracy, all about the economic wellbeing of the populace. This is why each EC, from the community to the national level, is preoccupied with identifying the economic needs of the people, which are articulated and aggregated into concrete policies of the government. This, in clear terms, is also economic nationalism because the underlining philosophy of Econocracy is an unrelenting pursuit of the economic prosperity of the populace.

The second plank of Ohno's feature of authoritarian developmentalism, which is obsession with external competitiveness under industrialization and export orientation, also applies to my Econocracy doctrine. As outlined earlier, the different national governments within the African region or the West African sub-region, as I shall amplify later in the next chapter, are designed to encourage and promote "external competitiveness and export orientation." In preceding chapters, I made the argument for regional market integration, driven by comparative advantage production lines. That is to say that each country within the region under competitive pressure, will find itself concentrating on areas of production where it has comparative advantage. With little or zero tariffs, export orientation is equally encouraged which in turn will encourage specialization and skill or technological advancement for higher production.

Finally, the feature on "top-down decision making under a powerful and economically literate leader and supporting elite group", finds clear expression in the structure of the ECs under Econocracy. Through the process of elections using the ECs as electoral colleges and with the provision of secretariats, those at state and national levels of the ECs made up of professionals and experts, those that emerge as the government operators are bound to be economically literate. The ECs at all levels, being their electoral base, equally provide a structure for top-down decision making, because the agenda or policies of government which are executed at the top also flow upward through inputs from the ECs. Also, without the distraction and encumbrances of partisan considerations, the government under econocracy is to be sufficiently powerful, to execute its programmes as it owes its survival and operational capability, not to the whims of political parties, but to the structure and support of the ECs and the populace.

Elaborating more on the role of the government in facilitating development, Ohno further outlined three essentials: the government, he says, must first create a market economy, because in the poorest or transition countries, domestic markets are extremely primitive. Given this primitive stage of the economy and the market, mere deregulation will be unable to unleash the latent market power to stimulate development. As a result, the government of such a country must constantly and flexibly mix market and government, in accord with its development stage. The second task for the government is to realize that putting in place the necessary rules, frameworks or laws for deregulation, privatization and free trade, although they are important, will not be enough on their own to stimulate growth. The government must, in addition, take necessary steps to encourage real sector concerns such as trade investment, technology and industrial structures, because competitiveness needs to be given vent through concrete content. The government should actively promote international integration, because as it happened in East Asia, economic development and external integration were two sides of the same coin and both proceeded in tandem. On the strength of the East Asia lesson, Ohno advised that "developing countries must design an integration timetable, which gives sufficient incentives for enterprise efforts by avoiding economic crisis and social instability. Here again, a delicate balance between liberalization and protection is required."

The third task is to mitigate the negative aspects of growth. In this respect, the government must find a way to manage the emerging income gaps among individuals, ethnic groups and regions as well as issues associated with urbanization like housing shortages and social evils, crime, corruption, drugs and prostitution. The government must curtail these negative fallouts from growth because economic development can only be sustained in an environment that promotes equity in the distribution of the fruits of, and opportunities from growth.

This is crucial because it is through such manifest equity that the virtuous circle of economic growth and social stability can be stimulated and sustained.

From the foregoing, it is my well-considered submission that Econocracy, if diligently executed, stands a good chance of replicating the miracle of the Asian Tigers in the African continent and the West African sub-region. There are yet other features that boosted the success of the Asian Tigers, which also reveal striking similarities with the Econocracy ideology.

Among other contributory factors to the high paced development of East Asia is education. Emphasis on education for both boys and girls, distinguished East Asia from the rest of the developing world by 1960. In the words of Ohno, "the levels of education and motivation in East Asia are among the many factors that have been cited to explain the rapid growth of the region." There is little doubt that mass education played a major role in the rapid development of East Asia. It was this policy that helped the labour force to adapt to new technologies that improved their productive skills. However, emphasis needs to be placed on the fact that a major stimulus to growth in the region, was its departure from the conditionality of international organizations. In this respect, it is instructive to recall that since 1999, the World Bank has insisted that poverty reduction was a necessary condition for the development of poor countries. Consequently, it directed all poor countries to draft a Poverty Reduction Strategy Paper (PRSP) as an essential tool of development. In line with this doctrine, the United Nations Millennium Summit held in September 2000, adopted the Millennium Development Goals (MDGs) for poverty reduction. This was a set of numerical social goals for poverty reduction by 2015. It is doubtful, however, that fifteen years after the MDGs, poverty has been reduced appreciably. If that was the case, Thousands of poor migrants from African and Arab countries will not be risking their lives every year trying to cross the Mediterranean Sea to Europe in search of better living conditions. According to Amnesty International, over 6000 people died in 2016 alone, trying to cross the Mediterranean to Europe. These were people who had been made so desperate by excruciating poverty that they consciously take the risk of drowning in the Mediterranean Sea while attempting to sail across. This was a preferred option, than to remain in their poverty ravished countries and die all the same, albeit a more humiliating death.

If the MDGs had significantly reduced poverty, about one hundred people would not have died in Ethiopia, as reported by all the major news agencies in the world, on March 12, 2017 at a landslide on a refuse dump, while scavenging for food from dumps. Evidence that poverty still persists in developing countries abound, which makes it more remarkable to note that no East Asian country adopted poverty reduction as major goal in national economic development. What they did was to adopt a more balanced approach to pursuing economic growth without losing sight of the need for social equity. The beauty of this approach is that it refused to limit itself to the narrow goal of poverty reduction as stimulus for growth. This approach appeals more to common sense wisdom because it should be obvious that there can be no real solution to poverty without sustained economic growth. This fact is demonstrated ever clearly as we look at the situation in Latin America, a region that has stuck to development through Western liberal ideology.

Latin America is a sharp contrast to East Asia. The twin evils of poverty and underdevelopment have dogged the region for many years. In his book, (Bulmer-Thomas, 1994), Victor Bulmer-Thomas aptly captured the pathetic tale of the region as follows: "The Economic History of Latin America Since Independence tells the story of promise unfulfilled. Despite the region's abundance of national resources and a favourable ration of land to labour, not a single republic in Latin America has achieved the stature of a developed country after nearly two centuries free of colonial rule."

The reality is that rather than develop, the gap between living standards in Latin American countries and the industrialized Western developed countries, whose ideology they emulate, has continued to widen. It may not be out of place to say that the development of Latin America began with its integration into world trading system centred on Europe and North America during the century before 1930. This, by implication, means that these countries accepted wholesale liberal ideology as a development model. This was made easier because most of the Latin American countries are located in the Western hemisphere. As identified by Bulmer-Thomas, the countries of Latin America are the ten republics of South America, excluding the three Cruianas and the six republics of Central America (including Panama, but excluding Belize). By this account, the countries will be twenty. However, my own count gives me twenty-one and they are: Argentina, Bolivia, Brazil, Chile, Cuba, Colombia, Dominican Republic, Ecuador, El-Salvador, Guatemala, Guyana, Haiti, Honduras, Mexico, Nicaragua, Panama, Paraguay, Peru, Uruguay and Venezuela.

The number may not be as important as the fact that these countries came from common historical background, which also shaped their approach to development. Like African countries, they were all colonized by Europe: namely Portugal and Spain. Majority of these countries gained independence from their colonial masters in the 1820s, thus making it almost two centuries of failed attempt at development.

As was almost the case in post independence Africa, the pattern of development in the nineteenth century was based on the export of natural resources to the industrialized countries. Although, by the time of independence, in the 1820s, standards of living were low in Latin American countries, they were not much lower than those of North America and were on a par with those of much of Central Europe. Yet after two centuries, the gap between the per capita income of Latin American countries and the industrialized Western countries has become so wide in favour of the industrialized countries that it becomes necessary to ask: what went wrong? The answer lies pointedly in the fact that Latin American countries bowed to the dictates of liberal development ideologies without relating them to their real economic needs and challenges. First, it was development through export of raw materials to industrialized countries; then came import substitution regimes, market-friendly policies, and export-led growth. All of these have come to naught, for, as Bulmer-Thomas observed, most of the Latin American countries have performed abysmally with respect to economic development. He reveals that the outcome is that the gap between income per head in Latin America and that in developed countries, notably the United States, is as wide as ever.

As earlier indicated, the major factor accounting for the poor development outing of Latin America can be traced to reliance on external development paradigm, namely those emanating from international organizations. This is vividly captured in the words of Bulmer-Thomas to wit: "The influence of the international context has always been of great importance for Latin America. However, the new wave of globalization – leading to the integration of product and factor market around the world – has increased the impact of the external environment on the region despite the reduced importance of primary products. Latin America is still struggling to find a way to maximize the benefits of globalization while minimizing the impact of negative external shocks. The dilemma has been harder by the decline in importance of an independent Latin American school of economic thinking. Most new ideas on economic policy now emanate outside the region and are adopted with only minor adaptations."

It is no surprise then that going by the 2020 world economic outlook as published by the international monetary fund (IMF), the total per capita income of just four Asian tigers namely; Taiwan - 55,078, Hong Kong - 64,927, South Korea - 44,740, and Singapore -103,180, making a total of 267, 925, is twice the total GDP of the 20 Latin American countries used for our analysis in this chapter, namely; Brazil - 6,450, Mexico - 8,069, Argentina - 8,433, Colombia - 5,207, Chile - 12,612, Peru - 5,845, Ecuador - 5,316, Dominican Republic - 7,445, Guatemala, 4,240, Uruguay - 15,335, Venezuela - 1,739, Bolivia - 3,322, Paraguay - 4,909, El Salvador - 3,821, Honduras - 2,412, Nicaragua - 1,832, Haiti - 732, and Guyana - 8,649, making a total of 106,365 USD. (*see tables 7 and 8*).

Table 7*: List of Asian countries by GDP per capita (Worldbank/ IMF)*

Territory	GDP Nominal Millions Of USD	GDP Nominal Per Capita USD	GDP PPP millions of USD	GDP PPP per capita USD
Total	31,582,000	7,351	65,441	15,235
Afghanistan	19,006	499	76,486	2,094
Bangladesh	317,768	1,888	837,588	5,028
China	14,860,775	10,839	27,308,857	19,503
Hong Kong	341,319	45,176	490,880	64,927
India	2,592,583	1,876	11,325,669	6,283
Indonesia	1,088,768	4,068	3,737,484	13,998
Iran	610,662	7,257	1,470,661	17,661
Iraq	178,112	4,438	705,059	18,025
Japan	4,910,580	39,048	5,888,913	46,827
North Korea	16,331	640	N/A	N/A
South Korea	1,586,786	30,644	2,319,585	44,740
Malaysia	336,330	11,136	1,078,537	32,880
Pakistan	284,214	1,388	1,202,091	5,871
Philippines	367,362	3,373	1,085,758	9,818
Singapore	337,451	58,484	585,055	103,180
Sri Lanka	81,120	3,689	304,826	13,897
Taiwan	635,547	26,910	1,300,212	55,078
Thailand	509,200	7,295	1,383,022	30,364
Timor-Leste	1,920	1,456	6.823	5,254
Turkey	649,436	7,715	2,346,576	28,264

Table 8: *List of Latin American and Caribbean countries by GDP per capita (Worldbank/IMF)*

S/N	Country	GDP (MILLIONS OF US$)	Per Capita Income ($)
1	Brazil	1,363,767	6,450
2	Mexico	1,040,372	8,069
3	Argentina	382,760	8,433
4	Colombia	264,933	5,207
5	Chile	245,414	12,612
6	Peru	195,761	5,845
7	Ecuador	93,078	5,316
8	Dominican Republic	77,883	7,445
9	Guatemala	76,191	4,240
10	Panama	60,286	14,090
11	Costa Rica	59,645	11,629
12	Uruguay	54,135	15,332
13	Venezuela	48,610	1,739
14	Bolivia	38,938	3,322
15	Paraguay	35,606	4,909
16	El Salvador	24,784	3,821
17	Honduras	23,984	2,412
18	Trinidad and Tobago	22,718	16,197
19	Jamaica	14,228	5,221
20	Nicaragua	11,905	1,832
21	The Bahamas	15,611.6	30,027
22	Haiti	8,347	732
23	Guyana	6,806	8,649
24	Barbados	4,630	16,082
25	Suriname	2,538	4,199
26	Saint Lucia	1,770	9,780
27	Belize	1,556	3,734
28	Antigua and Barbuda	1,389	14,159
29	Grenada	1,074	9,824
30	Saint Kitts and Nevis	871	15,246
31	Saint Vincent and the Grenadines	777	7,033
32	Dominica	545	7,709

The most interesting revelation is that total income per capita of 106,365 of the 20 Latin American countries is about the equivalent of the GDP of Singapore alone, which is 103,180. Nothing can define the excruciating poverty of these countries better than these sordid statistical figures.

From these statistics, it is clear that the country with the highest per capita income in Latin America, which is Uruguay, $15,332, is below the levels of Europe's lowest ranking countries such as Portugal with per capita income of $28,590. She is also four times lower than the per capita income of the US and three times lower than the European average. When you add these gaps to that revealed between Latin America and East Asia, it becomes crystal clear that the existing wealth gap between the industrialized countries and Latin America is truly very wide indeed. This is a firm confirmation that Latin American development efforts have failed, while that of the East Asian countries have recorded incredible success.

This is the lesson we must put to record as evidence that a wholesale importation of an external development model does not help the development needs of importer country. Further evidence of this can be discerned from the experience of Vietnam and the South East Asian region. The country has tried without success to use externally imposed conditionalities as a stimulant for development. This accounts for why she continues to lag behind in the development ranking of Asian countries with one of the lowest per capita income of just $2,777 and ranking 36th in Asia.

This is a partial list of Asian countries by GDP per capita at purchasing power. All figures are from the IMF and World Bank, 2020 economic outlook. The conclusion from the analysis of Latin American countries by per capita income is that the region is indeed poor and undeveloped.

Chapter 8

ECONOCRACY AS CENTREPIECE OF AFRI-DEMOCRACY

This book has tried to explain why African countries have remained underdeveloped half a century after independence, and in addition, formulated a development paradigm, that can develop the continent at a much faster pace than ever. This is a very tall ambition and I make no pretence whatsoever that my formula holds the miraculous key to the development of Africa. What I have done, which can stand the test of time, is use the tool of history, to explain how social forces can shape the institutions of nations for development purposes, and how an interpretation of the interplay of those forces, can be used to formulate a development paradigm for a given nation or region. Acemoglu and Robinson agree (429) that history can be a tool that shapes institutional trajectory of nations.

It is these trajectories that cumulated into the different models of development by nations or regions. In Western

Europe and North America, the outcome was liberalism, which, as an epoch in their historical process, gave birth to the model for parts of South-East Asia, namely China. In other parts of South-East Asia, economic nationalism and regional integration defined the path of development. In Africa and Latin America, a dependency syndrome, a by-product of colonialism, took the lead in shaping the post independent model that has defined efforts at economic growth in these regions.

As we saw in the course of the book, the historical trajectories of Western Europe, North America and East Asia, which culminated in liberalism, socialism and economic nationalism respectively, were responses to the historical forces that shaped the destiny of these regions. Liberalism facilitated development in the Western hemisphere, but communism did not do the same for China. This suggests rightly that these development models alone do not guarantee success or failure in national development. There are basic features that must be present in a political system for a model to make a success or failure of development. This will include a strong state structure and a virile cohesive society that can enforce accountability of the government to the populace. We already met these features in our previous chapters, which we described as an eternally vigilant populace and an ever alert political leadership. It is this balance between an eternally vigilant populace and an ever alert political leadership that makes for the success or failure of development in a nation.

The liberal democracies of the West have this balance, just like the East Asian countries. African countries lack both, owing mainly to their colonial history, which has made the state not just an instrument of subjugation and oppression, but vulnerable to ethnicity, religion and other divisive tendencies. The failure of the government to improve on the living conditions of the people, has ensured a disconnect between the government and the populace.

Econocracy is an attempt to use the ideology of economic determinism and nationalism to remedy the situation by creating the enabling environment for the emergence of a strong state and a virile, cohesive populace. As earlier noted, Econocracy is economic democracy. This implies using the economic interests of the people to define the political direction of the state. This can also be seen as economic determinism – that is, using economic interest to determine the political direction of the state. My argument is that this is the best approach for the speedy actualization of African development. This is justified on the grounds that this ideology should be seen as an appropriate response to the historical and sociological realities of post-colonial Africa. In this respect, Econocracy should be seen for what it is,

Afridemocracy for development. Put simply, it is the formulation of a peculiar democratic model that can facilitate development in Africa. As I argued in my book, (Emelumba, Reinventing Nigeria: The Plebiscitarian Option, 2016), democracy is a dynamic ideology that has continued to undergo variations and adaptations from continent to continent, since it first began in the Greek city state. The essence is for each environment to adopt the ideology of examples of democracy in a way that suits its own history and social realities. The examples of China and North Korea prove that a closed political system does not foster development. It was until China opened up its system through political reforms that it began to record substantial development. That reform involved an electric mix of Marxism and Western liberalism to suit China's peculiar circumstances. This is what adaptation is about, and Econocracy is the proposed African version of that adaptation with the following characteristics: guided deregulation to strike a balance between liberalism and protectionism, commitment to development of skills, technology, promotion of flow of investment, capital growth, job creation and development of regional markets.

We have touched on some of these points in previous chapters; it is necessary that for emphasis, we isolate them and examine them in more detail, as the underpinning philosophy of Econocracy.

Guided Deregulation

We envisage a situation where the government should guide a deregulation process to strike a balance between liberalism and protectionism. We have seen that unbridled deregulation of the market in accordance with the conditionality of international organizations, does not necessarily stimulate economic growth. This is so because the macroeconomic environment of an underdeveloped economy requires that the government should guide deregulation to achieve the desired result of development. Government policy should be to encourage deregulation to meet the needs of each stage of development. At the initial stage, the emphasis should be to encourage a productive process for a regionally integrated market. This will entail encouraging production in areas of comparative advantage in each country in the region, through different incentives such as tax breaks and zero tariffs.

However, care must be taken to ensure that the region is protected against influx of finished goods from advanced economies, whose products may come in better and cheaper against locally produced goods. The West African sub-region can be a good example in this respect. The countries in the sub-region can integrate their market, encourage competition among themselves along areas of comparative advantage, while protecting themselves from unbalanced competition with advanced economies. Specific areas where this can succeed include agriculture, staple food products, processed food and fruits, the footwear and textile industry, cosmetics and beauty products, etc. These are areas where the countries can specialize and produce goods and services for the regional market under a free trade arrangement, while protecting the influx of similar products from advanced economies. Later, as the countries consolidate and improve on their production, skills and technology, the market can be further opened to global competition.

Development of Skills/Technology

The governments should embark on massive skill acquisition and technology development programmes. I outlined how this can be achieved in chapter six of this book. Through this programme, skill efficient graduates are encouraged to start up their own enterprise in agriculture and agro-allied industries, footwear and garment industries and many others. Over time, their firms will improve on technology and become more efficient in production. The overall production capacity of the country will improve and expand, leading to more job opportunities and general economic growth.

Stimulation of Investment Flow

Using the National Development Bank of each country, in collaboration with the African Development Bank (AfDB), conscious effort will be made to encourage flow of investment into the market. Young entrepreneurs with bright ideas will be availed soft loan facilities, sourced from national and international financial institutions, to invest in different areas of the economy. This should be the main task of these banks. The focus should be to raise credible, visionary African entrepreneurs or capitalists, that can invest in production to stimulate growth, create employment opportunities, and grow the economy.

Job Creation and Capital Growth

A combination of the skill acquisition programme and the investment flow programme of the banks will certainly lead to job creation and capital growth. The effect of setting up young and brilliant graduates of skill acquisition in small and medium enterprises, is a generation of self-employment and general employment opportunities. In like manner, the inflow of investment from the development banks will grow local capital capacity and produce new African capitalists that will drive the national and regional economy.

Regional Markets

Each sub-region in Africa – West, East, North and South – can first develop their continental markets. Later, as they stabilize, an African regional market can then be created before going into the global market. While the sub-regions are at different stages of their integration, a charter of economic cooperation amongst them can still be worked out so that the sub-region can yet buy into each other's areas of economic strength and advantage.

Social Mobilization for Equity

All the above characteristics are designed to empty into one central agenda: social mobilization for equity. As we have seen, the colonial experience severed Africa from her path of economic development. Africa was moving on along a path of economic development before the advent of colonialism. Following the truncation of this path, Africans abandoned their locally made products ever since. More devastating however is the use of government apparatus to brutally subjugate Africans to the status of second class people. We saw how the instruments of state, such as the police, were used to achieve this during colonialism. This made the average African see the machinery of government as that of oppression and subjugation, leading to a near total distrust of government as an institution. That perception did not change with independence. Most Africans have remained disconnected from their government as a result.

The paradigm of Econocracy is designed to uproot this perception from the mentality of the African by making the people see themselves as truly part of the government. This is what the Economic Councils are designed to achieve. That the ECs will start from the community level, where every community is involved in determining and promoting its economic needs, is to ensure a re-enactment of faith of the people in the government. When the people at each community level become part of the process of deciding what the agenda of government should be, their attitude to, and perception of, a government is bound to change for good.

Besides, as members of the ECs, they are implicitly members of the government. They are bound to be more confident in the government as truly belonging to the people. I am certain that this is a good social mobilization process that can make the people truly part of the government.

Again, the fact that the economic agenda of the government is drawn from those needs identified and articulated from the community EC level, ensures that there is a sense of equity among the people in the distribution of public values. The diligent way this programme has been outlined for execution will also ensure that before the end of the ten-year tenure of a local, state/regional and national government, every community would have been touched one way or another. This also guarantees some sense of equity.

More importantly, the entire doctrine of Econocracy is woven around providing job opportunities, education, good health, and social infrastructure. Equity will definitely be served through this process as the different ethnic, religious and other divides in a country will be carried along in government. It appears conclusive, from all these, that Econocracy will encourage social, political, and economic mobilization of the people and that the cause of equity shall be served in the process.

Econocracy as the centrepiece of Afridemocracy, is a formulation that takes into due cognizance the historical realities of the continent as well as the political challenges of postindependence, which was practically stagnated growth. In a way, it can be seen as an African version of democracy, designed primarily to actualize development, more than for the upholding of the fine tenets of liberalism. The basic ingredients of Western democracy are there alright, but not at the same proportion or emphasis as liberal democracy. For instance, such expectations as periodic elections are there but the mode and process of elections vary dramatically. This is for the obvious reason which we noted earlier that the divisiveness and avoidable expenditure that come with elections in liberal democracies does not help Africa's development needs. To put it simply, Econocracy is formulated as an African democratic model for accelerated development in the continent, more than any other consideration.

Critics are bound to wonder how practicable this

formulation is. In other words, is this a mere utopian paradigm that is unworkable? I shall attempt to answer this in the next and concluding chapter.

Chapter 9

IS ECONOCRACY WORKABLE?

I know that quite a good number of people may be tempted to dismiss my proposition in this book as utopian or just impracticable. But I also know that most of the ideas that have changed the course of world history were initially dismissed as untenable. In the medieval era, many people and indeed most of the nations of the world were initially sceptical about the workability of democracy. The monarchies of the day rebuffed the idea of a democratic society and even resisted its advent.

It took a chain of events, spanning many years, to turn things around, starting from Europe. After a stiff operation by the monarchs, all the empires caved in and democracy had its way. But not as practised today.

The democratic system continued to progress, from different primitive stages such as Male suffrage to property suffrage to the present-day full-blown adult suffrage. Even the present-day separation of powers that is the best textbook definition of democracy, was a later day product of the continuous fine tuning of the system.

Ordinarily therefore, I would have simply submitted that an uncommon idea such as Econocracy, as proposed in this book, should be left for time to prove its practicability or not in Africa. But I refuse to be so persuaded for two reasons.

The first is that my intense interest in the study of politics and democracy leaves me in no doubt that Liberal democracy is only practicable in western countries. I believe that the reasons for this conclusion have been sufficiently adduced in this book and in my two other books: *Reinventing Nigeria, The Plebiscitarian Option* and *Election Finance and Corruption in Nigeria, An Investment Theory Approach.*

However, suffice it to add that even with all the necessary social factors in place in western countries for democracy to flourish, such as high literacy level, above poverty line per capita income and strong institutions. The 2020 elections in the United States clearly point to the fact that democracy is not the perfect system many think it is, even in the West.

Years ago, it would have been unthinkable to imagine that there could be an elected President of the United States who will refuse to concede defeat in a re- election bid. But not only did Donald Trump do so, he was able to convince millions of Americans that the election was fraudulently stolen from him. So much so that a multitude of them were ready to help Trump get back power by force.

The violent attempt by extremists to stop the United States Congress from certifying the election of Joe Biden as the 46th President of the United States will remain a sore point in the history of American democracy. It stands as a breathing indicator that even the presumed most secured democracy in the world is not immune to threats that can even crumble its foundations.

But the real implication here, is that Africa will be guilty of self-delusion to continue to imagine that it will find safety and economic development through western democracy.

The American unthinkable only makes it more cogent for Africa to find her own home-grown model of governance that can guarantee her security and development. This is imperative because the lesson for the continent from the United States January 6 'black democracy' day is that periodic elections, which is often the hallmark of democracy, but emotive and divisive, is not suitable for a backward African continent with low literacy level, wide spread poverty and insecurity, in addition to the near absence of relevant institutions that can serve as resilient valves against democratic head winds. In this respect, Econocracy recommends itself as a viable option.

The Second reason is borne out of my own curiosity to find out if indeed the concept of Econocracy is workable. This curiosity drove me into a field of experimentation which I am glad to share here.

In 2018, a year before the general elections in Nigeria, I decided to put my Econocracy theory to practical test. As a practising politician myself and as one who has contested for elections in the past, it was not difficult to push my experiment through. I called for a meeting of politicians and technocrats from my electoral ward, Ubulu, in Oru West local government area of Imo state. I solicited their cooperation to form a non-political, non-partisan group to be known as Ubulu Stakeholders Forum (USF).

I explained to them that the aim was to form a pressure group that will articulate, promote, and defend the political needs of the town. Our duty would be to identify the economic needs of the ward and prioritise them and keep them ready as a shopping list we shall present to politicians when they come looking for our votes. For instance, if from our shopping list, a health centre, a good road, or portable water is our priority for that election season, we shall present same to the different political party candidates that come to canvas for our votes as what we want them to do for us. In other words, we will not wait for them to tell us what they will do for us but will instead tell them what we want them to do for us.

For the candidates who agree to execute our demands, we shall make them commit to a signed agreement or contract. The summary of the contract is that we give you our votes and you do this and that for us without fail.

It becomes the responsibility of the USF thereafter to convince the voters to vote for the candidate who commits to the agreement. In the likely event that all candidates agree, out of the desire for victory, then USF will examine their credentials and settle for whoever they consider most dependable.

It was interesting to watch the reaction of those present at the meeting. Some raised salient questions such as what if a candidate reneges after committing to the agreement? What is the guarantee that the politicians will even agree to sit down and talk with us in the first place? Afterall they know that what matters on election day is not an agreement but how much money they can afford to give to the voters.

There was also the fear expressed by some as to whether the Forum can have a hold on the poor illiterate voter in the village who sees an election as an opportunity to extract his or her pound of flesh from the politicians, who they do not trust anyway.

All these concerns raised were quite germane and worrisome. But I tried as hard as I could to address them. Yes, a politician can renege after the agreement but that will be at his or her own peril and that of his political party. It means that we can blacklist both the politician and his party in subsequent elections. Those who refuse to negotiate with us will not get our votes. It is as simple as that.

But the tricky one was the assurance of having a hold on the voters. Truth to tell, the average Nigerian voter will stop at nothing to exchange his or her votes for money on election day. For them, the politician never keeps to his promises once elected.

The people believe that it makes no sense to listen to the litany of promises or even hold on to an agreement that will never be kept. For them, what is important is to use the opportunity of the election to make as much money as possible and never bother to expect democracy dividends from the politicians.

However, I explained that be that as it may, it should not stop us from trying. Afterall, like the saying goes, Rome was not built in a day. So, I believe that if we start and the people see the sincerity in the mission, more so when we are not asking them to vote for us, but to vote for those we have an agreement with for the good of the town, they may be persuaded.

Yes, it may take some time to get majority of the voters buy into the project but if we push consistently and passionately and the people see sincerity in what we are saying and doing, many of them are more likely to be converted.

In the end, the general consensus was that it was a brilliant idea worth pursuing. The USF was therein formally formed, and officials elected. A few weeks later, I invited leaders from the ward for the formal inauguration of the Ubulu Stakeholders Forum where I delivered a speech on the objectives of the Forum. The applause that greeted my speech said it all: USF was a very welcome development.

Thereafter, and ahead of the 2019 general elections, I mobilised the officials to immediately commence an enlightenment campaign in the town. This took them on visits to traditional rulers and union Presidents of the town.

Reports I got from the visitations further confirmed that the whole concept of the USF went down well with the people. It was a noble idea that the people did not only welcome but looked forward to its implementation.

At this point, having seen that the people welcomed the idea of originating a list of their wants from the government, I had to tactically withdraw from funding the organisation. I did so because I knew from day one that I couldn't afford to shoulder the logistics for carrying the organisation all through. This would require continuously funding a public enlightenment campaign that could take months and a lot of resources.

Even if I could afford to sponsor it in the short run, I will not be able to sustain a long run campaign which was crucial. So, I had to stop. But by then I had already gotten the result of the experiment I put in place, which was to find out if the theory of Econocracy was workable.

The amazing thing was that after discussing with members of USF, it was agreed that the most important needs of the people were economic. Among the first priority items in the first shopping list drawn up by the Forum were employment opportunities for graduates from the ward, good roads to link the town to the highways for ease of transportation of agricultural products and incentives for subsistence farmers.

This is the crux of the gospel of Econocracy: Letting the people seamlessly determine their economic needs having the power to enforce same as the agenda for government, without going through western type of democratic elections that alienates the voter from the government.

The general scepticism of the voter against the government as expressed in the USF meeting further amplify the above submission. So, on this score, I reached the conclusion that Econocracy is workable.

On another note, there is an interesting development in the World Bank circle on participatory budgeting for developing countries. It is called people's budget. The entire concept further amplifies the desirability of Econocracy.

The import of the people's budget concept is best captured in the article by Brautigam, 2004. The Kernel of his submission can be taken from the opening quote of the write up: "Recent moves towards participatory budgeting have raised hopes and expectations that spending and revenue generation can be made more pro-poor if informed citizens and their non-traditional political organisations participate directly in budgeting decisions."

This article reviews experiences of participatory budgeting and pro-poor policy making in Brazil, Ireland, Chile, Mauritius and Costa Rica. It draws attention to several important issues: Who participates? What kind of institutional framework is necessary? What happened to the revenue generation side of pro-poor budgeting?

It points out that making spending and taxation more pro-poor has historically depended on pro-poor political parties coming to power.

I will pick just an aspect of the findings of Bräutigam's work which clearly illustrate the efficacy of our Econocracy paradigm.

It proved that in Porto Alegre in Southern Brazil, participation by poor citizens, through parallel groups set up outside the normal channels of government (such as the Ubulu Stakeholders Forum) can yield better dividends of democracy.

The study specifically revealed that in Porto Alegre, the participatory budgeting process began with the PT organising two rounds of assemblies to gather demands of individual citizens and mobilise the community to select regional delegates. These delegates eventually elaborate in debates with the Mayor's technical officers, decisions on investment spending for the municipality, which are embedded in the Budget that the Mayor's office presents to the chamber.

The outcome in Porto Alegre has been impressive. As the World Bank reported: Between 1989 and 1996, the number of households with access to water services rose from 80% to 98%, percentage of the population served by the municipal sewage system rose from 40% to 85%, number of children enrolled in public schools doubled.

In the poorer neighbourhood, 30 kilometres of roads were paved annually since 1989 and because of transparency affecting motivation to pay taxes, revenue increased by nearly 50%"

From the above, the only difference between the above account and our Econocracy proposition is that in the Econocracy postulation, the people who assemble to propose items for government implementation, or budget, if you will, choose from among themselves those to be in the government proper. That is, those to implement the decisions agreed on. This is the only missing link.

The takeaway from the two illustrations I have provided above is that Econocracy is workable. One of the ways to begin is by forming political parties that believe in the Econocracy ideology. In that case, such political parties will go out to the field and canvas for votes on the ideology of Econocracy. This can be a good starting point which can thereafter blossom into full-fledged Econocracy. I submit thereafter that econocracy is indeed doable.

REFERENCES

Acemoğlu, D., & Robinson, J. A. (2012). *Why NAtions Fail.* New York: Crown Pubishing Group.

Africa Kitoko. (2020, July 4). *Life expectancy in Africa.* Retrieved from Africa Kitoko: https://africakitoko.com/life-expectancy-in-africa/

Bentham, J. (1789). *An Introduction to the Principles of Morals and Legislation.* London: Printed for T. Payne and Son at the Mews Gate.

Bräutigam, D. (2004). The People's Budget? Politics, Participation and Pro-poor Policy. *Developmenet Policy Review*, 22(6), 16.

Bulmer-Thomas, V. (1994). *The Economic History of Latin America Since Independence.* Cambridge: Cambridge University Press.

Charles R. Mayes, *The Sale of Peerages in Early Stuart England* The Journal of Modern History, Vol. 29, No. 1 (Mar., 1957), pp. 21-37. Published By: The University of Chicago Press.

Cranston, S. R. (1979). Regulating Business: Law and Consumer Agencies. London: Palgrave Macmillan.

Earle, J. Moran, C. & Ward-Perkins, Z. (2017). *The Econocracy: The Perils of leaving Economics to the Experts.* Penguin.

Emelumba, D. M. (2016). *Reinventing Nigeria: The Plebiscitarian Option.* London: Strategic Books Publishing and Rights Agency (SBPRA) .

Emelumba, D. M. (2017). *Election Finance and Corruption in Nigeria: An Investment Theory Approach.* London: Strategic Books Publishing and Rights Agency (SBPRA).

Ferguson, A. (1767). *An Essay on the History of Civil Society.* Edinburgh: Printed for A. Millar & T. Caddel and A. Kincaid & J. Bell.

Ferguson, J. (1994). The Anti-Politics Machine: *Development, Depoliticization, and Bureaucratic Power in Lesotho.* Minneapolis: University of Minnesota Press.

Fukuyama, Y. F. (1992). *The End of History and the Last Man.* New York: Free Press.

Kamili, Z. (2011). *The History of Africa from 1880 to Present.* Dar es Salaam: KOT Publishers.

Kato, B. H. (1975). *Theological Pitfalls in Africa.* Kisimu: Evangelical Publishing House.

MacDonogh, G. (1999). Frederick the Great: *A Life in Deed and Letters.* London: Weidenfeld.

Makherjee, S., & Ramaswamy, S. (2007). *A History of Political Thought: Plato to Marx.* New Delhi: Prentice-Hall of India Private Limited.

Mbachu, O. (1998). Education, Politics, and Illusion: *The Arguments of a Political Theorist*. Owerri: Kosoko Press Ltd.

Mimiko, N. O. (2017). *Democradura: Essays On Nigeria's Limited Democracy*. North Carolina: Carolina Academic Press.

Montesquieu, C. D. (1748). The Spirit of Laws. Geneva: Barrillot & Fils.

Ogwumike, F. O. (1995). *The Effects of Macrolevel Government Policies on Rural Development and Poverty Alleviation in Nigeria*. Ibadan Journal of the Social Science, 85-101.

Ohno, K. (2002, August 8). *The East Asian Experience of Economic Development and Cooperation*. Tokyo, Japan: National Graduate Institute for Policy Studies (GRIPS).

Okonjo-Iweala, N. (2012). *Reforming the Un-reformable: Lessons from Nigeria*. Cambridge: The MIT Press.

Rodney, W. (1972). *How Europe Underdeveloped Africa*. London: Bogle-L'Ouverture Publications.

Rousseau, J. J. (1754). *Discourse on Inequality*. Amsterdam: Marc-Michel Rey.

Rousseau, J. J. (1762). *The Social Contract*. Amsterdam: Marc-Michel Rey.

Smith, A. (1776). *The Wealth of Nations*. London: W. Strahan and T. Cadell.

Self, P. (1975). *Econocrats and the Policy Process: Politics and Philosophy of Cost-benefit Analysis*. Macmillan.

Tocqueville, A. d. (1856). *The Old Regime and the Revolution* (1st ed.). New York: Harper & Brothers, Publishers.

Voltaire, A. d. (1733). *Letters on the English*. Paris: Basile.

Voltaire, A. d. (1764). *Philosophical Dictionary*. Geneva: Gabriel Grasset.

www.ingramcontent.com/pod-product-compliance
Lightning Source LLC
Chambersburg PA
CBHW041214030426
42336CB00023B/3343